Through GATES of PEARLS

A Personal Roadmap To Glory

EVERSEL M. GRIFFITH

Copyright © 2014 EMG PUBLICATIONS

Copyright ©2014 EMG Publications
ALL RIGHTS RESERVED

PUBLISHER'S NOTE

This is a work of non-fiction. Names, characters, places, and incidents are the author's translation and quotation of Scriptures from the various Bibles as indicated, and personal life experiences and insights. Public Domain.

No portion of this book publication may be reproduced, stored in any electronic system, or transmitted in any form or by any means, electronic, mechanical, photocopy, recording, or otherwise, without the written permission EMG Publications.

CopyRight Number: **1-1549986621**

Library of Congress Control Number:

ISBN: **978-0-9826895-3-0**

- All Scripture quotations, unless otherwise noted, are taken from *KJV,* the **King James Version** of the Bible.
- Scripture quotations marked *AMP* are taken from the **Amplified Version.**.
- Scripture quotations marked *ASV* are taken from the **American Standard Version**.
- Scripture quotations marked *HCSB* are taken from **Holman Christian Standard Bible**.
- Scripture quotations marked *NASB* are taken from the **New American Standard Bible**.
- Scripture quotations marked *NASU* are taken from the **New American Standard Bible Updated Edition**.
- Scripture quotations marked *NIV* are taken from the **New International Version**.
- Scripture quotations marked *NKJV* are taken from the **New King James Version**.
- Scripture quotations marked *NLT* are taken from the **New Living Translation**.
- Scripture quotations marked *RSV* are taken from the **Revised Standard Version**.
- Scripture quotations marked *TLB* are taken from **The Living Bible**.
- Scripture quotations marked *Phillips* are taken from **J.B. Phillips New Testament**.

Cover Design & Layout by: www.**RepromanProductions.com**

PRINTED IN THE UNITED STATES OF AMERICA

TABLE OF CONTENTS

INTRODUCTION v

Chapter: 1
THE JOURNEY - AN INTRICATE ROAD 1

Chapter: 2
SUBMISSION 13

Chapter: 3
DESTINY HINDRANCES 27

Chapter: 4
HOPE 43

Chapter: 5
DOORWAYS TO THE SOUL 57

Chapter: 6
CLOSING DOORWAYS 77

Chapter: 7
WHO SPEAKS INTO YOUR LIFE? 89

Chapter: 8
EFFORT, NOT PERFECTION 101

Chapter: 9
WOUNDED IN THE HOUSE OF MY FRIENDS 111

Chapter: 10
HOLY SPIRIT ORCHESTRATED REVIVAL 125

Chapter: 11
HOLINESS HIGHWAY 139

Chapter: 12
THE VALLEY OF TEMPTATION 161

Chapter: 13
PRAYER & FAITH LANES 173

Chapter: 14
TO THE GATES OF PEARLS 191

Chapter: 15
THE VICTORIOUS BRIDE 201

Also Available from EMG Publishing 219

INTRODUCTION

This book is an effort to provide encouragement, awareness and stability as you journey from earth to heaven. In it, I will highlight some of the pitfalls, distractions and precautions you need to be aware of along the way. As a Christian, this information will be meaningful to you. To many, it will be a priceless treasure that aides and seals their successful run to heaven's gates.

Revelation, the book that details the final events of our world system, speaks of the *Gates of Pearls* as the exuberant entrance to heaven – *Revelation 21:21*. If you have not heard about these gates, get ready for a pleasant awakening. You may experience some uneasiness as you walk with me through some rugged terrain, but I'll try to warn you when to fasten your seatbelt.

If you have been a Christian for some time, you should know by now that the Christian's life has challenges. In case no one explained this to you before, this journey calls for commitment and much personal sacrifice. Jesus challenged all who would follow Him to deny themselves, take up their cross and follow Him daily. I will share some personal experiences of challenges and miracles I have experienced, but I'll tell you very bluntly about the inflexible requirements for entrance to heaven. I'll address various Christian personalities and some areas may be very thought provoking. Step up to the challenges I will present however, and consider any uncomfortable sections as my sincere desire to help you reach heaven. This book is one of God's ways of showing how much He loves you and wants you to run a successful race to the place Jesus has prepared for you.

Christianity is a religion of choice. Adherents are free to walk away at any time. Like most other volunteer institutions, members exercise various levels of commitment to its rules. So, whatever level you have committed to, most likely I'll challenge you to raise it *(maybe)* many notches. **Salvation is free**, *but making it to the* **Gates of Pearls** *necessitates effort on your part.* I won't promise you a *"pie in the sky"* or a *"bed of roses"* on your way there. Especially in the days ahead, expect difficulties and challenges. Often, you will be tempted to turn back and some trials will seem long. At times, burdens will become heavy and criticism may launch at you from the least expected areas. Betrayal by trusted friends or family may try to knock you off your feet as well.

This book may find you at a crossroad where the road seems so rocky and overwhelming, you are crying in silent despair. It may have dropped into your hand as you wrestle with thoughts of surrendering to the tide that's rushing across the highway and has forced you to a screeching halt. It may have found you at your highest moment or at your lowest low. If it finds you at your high point, bask in the sunshine and gloat in your reprieve, but don't stop to pick flowers. Admire them only as you run as fast as you can to make up for the time you will relish in the deep valleys and steep hills up ahead...

Run! Run fast! Run like never before.

If this book finds you at your lowest, keep your eyes on the prize - the prize at the *Gates of Pearls*. Allow me to speak into your life. It'll do you much good to sit and listen attentively. I understand your predicament, but no! I will not join you on your seat of despair; not even to comfort you. I may extend my hand for you to grab, and I will pull as hard as I can to help you on your journey, but I will not join you. I will challenge you to get up and start running again.

Lower your head before the King of Kings and let me bless you as you begin this book.

Your Blessing

May blessings from God overtake you from the moment you begin reading this book.

May your journey through life be filled with a great and certain expectancy of entering through the Gates of Pearls.

May you receive all the support you need to reach this goal.

May everything that rises to defeat you fall in defeat before your feet.

May the Lord's presence be with you always; encouraging you, strengthening you and helping you to enter the city of God.

May the Lord Jesus stand at the gate with open arms to welcome you along with many of those you have helped along the way.

May you stand with all the saints of the ages, dressed in white linen robes, knowing that you fought a good fight and kept the faith.

Your Friend in Christ,
Eversel Griffith
Prophet Ezekiel
Email me at **EgMtcarmel@aol.com**

To get the maximum from this book, read it in a quiet place.

Feel free to use this material for Bible study.

Also, use it as a reference to aid in developing your Christian faith.

CHAPTER 1
THE JOURNEY
AN INTRICATE ROAD

You have embraced Christianity. You believe you are on the journey that leads from earth to heaven. You believe you are on your way to streets of gold. You have repeated the sinners' prayer and joined the Church. Is it really that simple? There are so many religions in the world today; almost all of them touting their way to heaven. How do we know which one is the right one? Even within the different factions of Christianity, there are varying beliefs regarding the path to the *Gates of Pearls*. Some of these beliefs are diverse enough to cause conflict, division and separation even within the same denomination. Yet, members from both sides believe that they are on the right path to heaven's streets of gold.

Since the Church's establishment, it has seen various transformations. It has seen hills, valleys, dormancy and revival. The reformation at the turn of the sixteenth century ushered the protestant movement. This movement resulted in the formation of Pentecostals, then Wesleyans, Methodist and other protestant denominations. Today, Christianity is realizing a new trend: Non denominational congregations who choose not to affiliate with any traditionally organized church.

So, where do you stand in this maze of religious infrastructure? Most likely, you feel passionate about your religious belief. Some Christians would rather backslide than to join a Church that is not part of their denomination. Yet, congregants from that other

Church are just as passionate about their beliefs. They believe that they are on their way to heaven as well. Some denominations believe that unless your church has a specific name you are doomed. Some believe that unless you are a member of their organization there is no hope for you. Some believe that you must speak in tongues to be saved. Some believe that you must be baptized in Jesus' name only.

- Can all of us be right and yet vary on so many issues?
- What if only one of all these denominations is right?
- What if the teachings we've embraced are in error?
- How can we be sure we are on our way to heaven?
- Is reaching heaven just a matter of belief or are beliefs critical for those who make it there?
- Will God look beyond the folly of our divided Christianity and accept all of us?
- How did we ever get in this mess anyhow?

The answers to these questions cannot be found within ourselves.

In fact, the look inward for such answers is the reason why there are so many religious splinters today. These divisions have also fueled much of the chaos the world is currently experiencing. I know this statement could meet with fierce opposition from our post modern religious culture, but there is enough evidence to support this hypothesis.

Post modern world culture propagates notions of self preservation, self interest and the superiority of human ability. The need for enforcing law and order however, demonstrates that if left to self-will and self-judgment, humans would wipe us off the planet in a short time. No! We cannot look within ourselves if we are looking for truthful answers to these pressing questions. We must look elsewhere.

Even as twenty-first century Christians, we cannot trust our own wisdom or values to ascertain the correct answers. Our values system has been so influenced by the world's ethics; we are unknowingly, but steadily adopting anti-Christian culture and principles. We are falling so far away from Godly morals; today's headlines are inundated daily with morbid stories of ungodly acts committed by Christians. Some tenured leaders are falling from grace and many of their congregants are mulling around in utter delusion. Some of these lost congregants have even backslidden.

- If many of our Christian leaders are failing, what values can they instill in us?
- How can we tell if the values they taught us were genuine?
- Were these values tarnished through their unholy living?
- Obviously, these leaders don't know the way to heaven, so where does that leave those who are following them?

No! We cannot look inside for answers because we may have been handed the wrong tools or erroneous information. We must look outside ourselves to find answers to these pertinent questions. We must conclude that the ideology of our Church Age has been discolored by modern culture. This cultural influence is so subtle, many Christians are not aware that they are thinking, acting and reacting more like the world instead of responding to life's issues the way followers of Christ should.

Jesus said that although we are in the world we are not of the world. To get through the Gates of Pearls we must be covered by the blood of Jesus and remain under that covering. We cannot straddle the fence, continue in our old ways and expect to remain under the blood covering. Jesus said in **John 15:4** –

> *"The branch cannot bear fruit of itself, except it abide in the vine; no more can ye, except ye abide in me."*

The road to the *Gates of Pearls* requires that *we first accept the blood of Jesus as our covering* and then remain under that umbrella by *consistently following and obeying the Lord Jesus*.

> *"For the life of the flesh is in the blood, and I have given it to you upon the altar to make atonement for your souls;* **for it is the blood that makes atonement for the soul**.*"*
>
> – **Leviticus 17:11** *(NKJV)* emphasis is mine

To reach the *Gates of Pearls* we must have them in our thoughts and envision them daily. The decisions we make must be influenced by this daily spiritual view of them. Our eventual entrance to the gates must affect all our actions. We must reject anything that would smear our view of them and grasp everything that would enhance our vision. All our actions must corroborate everything that would aide our entrance to the golden gates that Christian patriots talked about so often.

Testimony In Song

How did they make it? What characteristic did they have that allowed those long gone generals of the Christian faith to run a successful race? We must walk daily with the Lord Jesus, just like those great patriots walked with Him. They have ran their race, reached the gates and have won their prize. I'm sure that for many of them, the road they travelled was treacherous and difficult at times:

> *"And what more can I say? Time is too short for me to tell about Gideon, Barak, Samson, Jephthah, David, Samuel, and the prophets, who by faith conquered*

kingdoms, administered justice, obtained promises, shut the mouths of lions, quenched the raging of fire, escaped the edge of the sword, gained strength after being weak, became mighty in battle, and put foreign armies to flight...

...and others experienced mockings and scourgings, as well as bonds and imprisonment. They were stoned, they were sawed in two, they died by the sword, they wandered about in sheepskins, in goatskins, destitute, afflicted, and mis-treated. The world was not worthy of them."

– **Hebrews 11:32-34 & 36-38** *(HCSB)*

- Adversity and trials are often our best instructors.
- Most of the Psalms were formed in the wilderness.
- Most of the Epistles were written in prison.
- Hymn writers taught in song what they gleaned from adversity.

As we reminisce through the great hymns of the Church, we see how various song writers lived and died. It was very brave of them to penn their hopes, their dreams and their experiences. They dare us now to follow in their footsteps if we aspire to join them on the glory shore.

Hymns are a dying part of worship in many churches today, but as we look at some of the lyrics, we see that the writers wrote with passion and resolve. They wrote with an assurance of seeing those golden gates and entertained nothing that would divert their focus. Some of them wrote so distinctly of heaven, they must have had glimpses of that land beyond the river. *Fanny J. Crosby* was blind, but you won't know this from her writings. She wrote descriptive scenes of heaven as if she had already seen it. She looked forward with enthusiasm to the day when she would see her

Lord and Savior *face to face.* Lest she should waver or stray from the path to glory, she embraced Calvary as the sure route to heaven and solemnly asked Jesus to keep her *"Near the Cross."*

As we think somberly on the words left by these long gone Christians, we see fervor in their resolve. We see a committed resignation to reaching the other side - a resignation that even the trials of life they were encountering could not deflate. Many of them had hard and difficult lives. Some experienced great pain and suffering, but in their songs, we hear them disparagingly questioning whether it was even Christianly ethical to expect to reach their heavenly destination on beds of ease, while others experienced significant trials and difficulties.

- Oh, that we would embrace the cross with the same genuine passion!
- Oh, that we would find the same solace in Calvary's cleansing stream!
- Oh, that our lives would be just as fragrantly, yet somberly graceful!
- Oh, that grace would flow from our lips as it flows from their testimonies in song!
- Oh, that we would run our race successful, see them and shake their now renewed hands!

"Since we have such a huge crowd of men of faith watching us from the grandstands, let us strip off anything that slows us down or holds us back, and especially those sins that wrap themselves so tightly around our feet and trip us up; and let us run with patience the particular race that God has set before us."

– Hebrews 12:1 *(TLB)*

Sister Myril

They called her Sister Myril or, just *Myril*. That's how the people in her community sarcastically and disrespectfully referred to her, but for us, she was Pastor Ifill - our pastor. I don't think she had more than a second grade education, but she was a hero. Our church had many families with children. Many of the children came to church only on special occasions, yet she knew all their names. She wrote poems for all the children and didn't re-use any of them. She wrote poems for the Easter program, the Christmas program and the Harvest program. Don't think you could trip her up by leaving out a portion of your recital if you had not memorized it thoroughly. She knew what she wrote. She wrote and directed all the church plays. She conducted all the rehearsals as well. She could have solicited help, but her standards were very high. She knew what she wanted and settled for nothing less than the best.

She saw clearly into the spirit realm. Once, our church visited a church in another part of the country. A member of that church stood up to testify. Our pastor told her to sit, but the lady refused and ostentatiously continued to share her testimony. Pastor Ifill told her sit down because she had fought with her mother-in-law that day. This lady accused her pastor of discussing her shortcomings with our pastor. But one didn't have to tell Pastor Ifill anything; she lived in the spirit realm.

She was ridiculed and heckled by the town's people because she dared to be different. She was resolute and unbending in her pursuit of holiness. She wanted nothing to do with anything that even had an inclination to offend God. Other churches would have annual fundraiser bus trips to parks and beaches, but not our church. Once, our church held an excursion and some of the patrons behaved unpleasantly. Pastor Ifill apologized to God and that was the last time our church held one.

She gave her life for the Church. She fasted one day a week for herself and Wednesday through Sunday she fasted for the Church. The congregation however, didn't appreciate all of her dedication and hard labor. Back then, a full time pastor lived off the tithes. Although the members knew this, most of them would put only a few silver coins in the tithes box. She fell sick, probably because of poor nutrition. She had a large congregation, yet she died in the poor house. She had a challenging life, but remained steadfast to the end. She was a hero. I believe she has passed those gates and that she is enjoying her great reward in heaven.

If we are to sit next to these successful Christian soldiers in their grandstand hall of fame, we must walk in their shoes, follow in their footsteps and embrace their resolve. We must clinch the same passionate desire they had for walking on the streets of gold and meeting the Savior by the river of life. We must envision the Savior in bright shining apparel and the one whom just seeing His face signals the end of the race, the exuberance of victory, and the exchange of our earthly bodies for glorified ones. Just like these triumphant forerunners, accolades or recognition in this life must not be on the forefront of our minds. We must count the cost and prepare to suffer if that's what it takes to see the Savior.

> *"Dear friends, don't be bewildered or surprised when you go through the fiery trials ahead, for this is no strange, unusual thing that is going to happen to you. Instead, be really glad-because these trials will make you partners with Christ in His suffering, and afterwards you will have the wonderful joy of sharing His glory in that coming day when it will be displayed".*

– 1 Peter 4:12-13 *(TLB)*

A Necessary Change

The Western Church is losing the battle in its quest to influence today's social and religious culture. Our world system *(greed, materialism and covetousness)* is steadily squeezing church etiquette out of its culture. In many communities, the Church is bending to this pressure and sacrificing Christian principles with the hope of re-attracting fans. A social gospel is therefore steadily replacing Spirit filled - Spirit led doctrine. The result is that many today have lost directions to heaven and are not even aware that they are lost.

Today's prevalent social gospel then, is birth out of the world system. Regretfully, its acceptance by the Church is gaining momentum. In many situations, the wisdom of the world is speaking louder than the wisdom of God's word because many Christians are not being fed the truth of God's word. That's why much of our thinking aligns with the world's mindset rather than the *Christ-like* demeanor we are expected to exhibit.

We are not suppose to think or react like the world. Just like our Lord and Savior Jesus, we are in the world, but we are not of the world. God expects us to be different, heaven expects us to be different and our Christian brothers and sisters expect us to be different. Even the prostitute on the corner and the addict in the abandon house down the street expect us to be different as well.

> *"This means that anyone who belongs to Christ has become a new person. The old life is gone; a new life has begun!"*

> **– 2 Corinthians 5:17** *(NLT)*

The world is also silently but desperately looking for this difference in Christians. On the job, fellow employees may talk about you and make fun of you because you claim to be *born again*. They don't invite you to their social gatherings because you are *"Sister Holy."* But who do they come looking for when sickness strikes their family or a loved one dies? You! Yes you, because they want someone they believe can get a prayer through. They are not just insensitive or godless; they are smarter and more knowledgeable of Godly principles than we credit them. They know who is living a Godly life. They have the understanding that trashy, uncommitted Christians won't be able to get answers they need from God. I wonder who taught them that?!!!

Christians are to be different.

After accepting Christ, we should exhibit a comprehensive change, but this change is not necessarily automatic. Some people experience a significant change when they receive Christ, while others realize only a small change. After we are *"born again"*, whether we experience a dramatic change or just a little, we are challenged to renew our mind. **Romans 12:2** challenges all Christians to *seek and embrace the mind of Christ*. If these guidelines were adhered to and practiced by Christians, this world would be a much nicer place. But have you noticed that even in the Church conflict is growing?

If a change is to occur in the Church, it will not begin at the corporate level. The change must take place first at an individual level before a change at the corporate level can be realized. Change must begin with you not necessarily with other Christians. Since we are not sure we have received the correct tools or the necessary vehicles to travel successfully, we must first seek truth.

The last thing we want is religion.

We need truth – we need a map with the proper directions to get us from here to the Gates of Pearls. Truth is that map and it is critical to reaching the gates.

"Buy the truth, and sell it not; also wisdom, and instruction, and understanding." – **Proverbs 23:23**

What is truth?

How important is it? Is it relative to what we believe? What we believe can either help us to reach heaven or cause us to miss it altogether. Religion is not necessarily truth. Truth leads us to heaven while religion leads us in the opposite direction. In **John 14:6** *(HCSB)*, Jesus said:

"I am the way, the truth, and the life. No one comes to the Father except through Me."

We must be honest and open to embrace truth whether it is revealed or taught to us. We must be committed to embracing truth so much as to recant our traditional or acquired religious beliefs, if they do not align with the principles that lead to the Gates of Pearls.

- Are you willing to take that step--to compare your religion with truths' guidelines to glory?
- Are you willing to sacrifice religion for a walk on the streets of gold?
- Are you willing to search your own heart to see if you are honest and open to truth?

These are tough questions for many, but it shouldn't be this way. The grip of religion however, is strong and overpowering. Often, people would rather hold on to their religion because it provides a self-justifying comfort zone. It makes them feel good about themselves. It allows them to bury their head in the sand and be oblivious to any external danger. Could your religion *(Christian or Non Christian)* fall into this category? I admire the person who is willing to compare his or her beliefs, traditions or even emotions with God's word and make appropriate decisions.

It is critical that we leave a legacy of truth; otherwise, the next generation will have to re-invent the wheel to find it. What we pass on to them is vital for their successful run to the *Gates of Pearls*. We must leave the correct tools for them, so that they can apply Godly principles to address the issues they will face. Let's seek truth and pass it on to them.

How To...

- Don't look within for truth; look outside; look to *Holy Spirit*.
- Even if you look to Christian leaders for directions, always seek God for confirmation.
- Keep the *Gates of Pearls* in your view daily and reject everything that would smear your vision of them.
- Don't try to reinvent the wheel. Glean from the lyrics of hymns and testimonies of others.
- Decide today that seeing the Lord Jesus Christ at the *Gates of Pearls* is worth sacrificing all earthly pleasures.
- Seek for truth, search God's word, seek God's face and you'll see the Gates of Pearls.

"For yourself, concentrate on winning God's approval, on being a workman with nothing to be ashamed of, and who knows how to use the word of truth to the best advantage."

– 2 Timothy 2:15 *(Phillips)*

CHAPTER 2
SUBMISSION

Judaism taught, *"An eye for an eye and a tooth for a tooth."* Although Christianity has its roots in Judaism, Christianity is very different from Judaism. Submission is an intricate part of Christianity which teaches us not to retaliate in kind to those who mistreat us. Jesus demonstrated this ideology by submitting to the cross and asked all His followers to turn the other cheek as well. To follow Jesus this way calls for submission. Our heart must also corroborate this resolve since no other part of us will. Submission must be our closest associate as we run the race to the *Gates of Pearls*. Of course, the type of submission being referred to here is the type that's congruent to God's word.

Submission entails obedience, surrendering and compliance to another person's ideology. This is not always easy. Especially today, Christ's call for submission collides with many of our cultural ideologies. God's word teaches us to submit to ordinances, but not to laws which infringe His principles. Our commitment to Him must surpass everything we do here on earth, even our own well-being. Since the Church began, many Christians suffered martyrdom because they ran into a head-on collision with the ordinances of the ruling authorities.

God's word asks that we submit to our church leaders, but we cannot truly submit to them until we become submissive to God. In **Genesis**, *Sarai* treated her servant *Hagar* very harshly. When

Hagar could no longer bear the harsh treatment, she ran away. The angel of God met her and told her, *"Return to your mistress, and submit to her authority"* – **Genesis 16:9**. He advised her not only to return, but to submit also. Many Christians find this kind of submission difficult. The Word may entreat them to return, but to submit to leadership; that's a different story. Submission is often very challenging, but we must be obedient to God. God knew that Sarai mistreated Hagar. He knew that Hagar was tired of being harassed, yet He told her to go back and submit to Sarai. Has God addressed you this way regarding some decisions you've made? How about reconciling with your *(ex)* and submitting?

Resolution of Submission

Authorities in China arrested two young women for their observance of the Christian faith. As these two young Christians sat in the back of the police car *(on their way to God knows where)*, they sang songs of praise and adoration to the Lord Jesus. The officer turned to them and said, *"You girls are crazy. Don't you know what is going to happen to you?"* They replied, *"You don't understand what an honor it is to suffer for Christ."* That is resolve! Are we there yet - to lay down our very lives for the Lord Jesus Christ without flinching? Obviously, these two young ladies had made their decision to suffer long before they were thrown into the back of the police car. Obviously, they were expecting this to happen at any time and they were prepared for it. They were prepared to stand firm in their faith even if doing so meant their death. I'm sure they had close friends and family; probably brothers and sisters, cousins, aunts, uncles, a mother and a father. For sure, they would not see them again. These two young Christians would have loved to be married, raise a family and vacation in New York City. However, they put aside all these earthly relationships and pleasures and made

the sacrificial decision that seeing the Lord Jesus Christ at the Gates of Pearls was priceless. Paul and Silas encountered similar circumstances and expressed the same resolve:

> *"And at midnight Paul and Silas prayed, and sang praises unto God: and the prisoners heard them".*
>
> **– Acts 16:25**

What kind of people were these two young women that they so casually but decisively made the decision to suffer? They were ordinary young women who in a quieter, peaceful, solemn, prior moment, made the decision to follow the Lord Jesus Christ regardless of future circumstances. Obviously, they were shown the possible dangers and challenges of such a path; yet they made the decision to follow Christ. From the moment they committed to that resolution, their entire lifestyle would reflect the decision they made that day. They lived everyday as their last. Most likely, they kissed or hugged loved ones every time they parted, knowing that it could be their last greeting on this side of heaven. When the day for them to suffer finally came, they didn't panic. They didn't cringe in fear, worrying if they would ever see their loved ones again. They had already made that decision and they were prepared. They were ready! Preparation is the key.

We must come to this same resolve before persecution reaches us. We must decide today for what tomorrow's shadows will bring. If we don't make this decision today, it will be difficult to make it when trouble comes. Our post modern culture is changing very fast. Morals are spiraling downward and liberal ideologies are receiving greater acceptance. People are caring more about material achievements than moral values. This liberal thinking has so infected our culture; it is impacting all levels of our judiciary.

Judeo-Christian ethics are under constant attack and we are losing freedom daily. Only God knows how long it will be before this atmosphere intensifies enough to dissipate all Judeo-Christian morals and outlaw Christian values entirely. This trend is moving subtly, but quicker than we think.

How would you react if you faced the same predicament that these two young Christians faced? I'm sure you would agree that many Western Christians would react very differently if faced with similar circumstances. What made the difference however, was preparation. The key element is making the decision now rather than later. We must make the decision today to prioritize seeing the *Gates of Pearls*. There are many dangers, toils and snares up ahead. We must decide *(now)* to put everything, everyone and even our own lives second to seeing the gates. This message of prioritizing our destiny needs to be echoed from every pulpit and every Christian radio and TV program. Everything that we do in Christendom should be secondary; even ministry. Seeing a smile of satisfaction on Jesus' face ought to be every Christian's ultimate goal. We must commit to this now!

Submission to Adversity

As seen by the young Chinese Christians, commitment does not change with circumstances. The circumstances did not change their decision. The free Church falls short in this level of commitment, yet this allegiance to Christ is the backbone of the Church. A commitment is very different from a promise, but many people do not understand this and break their vows when conditions change. The divorce rate today is a prime example of this, yet every marriage begins with a solemn vow to stay together until death. They call it a vow but the rate of divorce contradicts this. A commitment is binding. It is synonymous to a covenant or contract. It rests on assurance, dedication, obligation, and loyalty.

Jesus made a commitment to come to earth, to suffer and be crucified for man's sin. The night before His great sacrifice, His human side cringed from the impending pain and suffering. In the Garden of Gethsemane He prayed:

> *"My soul is exceeding sorrowful, even unto death: tarry ye here, and watch with me. And He went a little farther, and fell on His face, and prayed, saying, O my Father, if it be possible, let this cup pass from me: nevertheless not as I will, but as thou wilt."*
> **– Matthew 26:38-39**

Every Christian begins this journey with a decision to follow Christ, but many turn away two minutes before adversity even shows is face. Many people start on this road with all good intentions of making it to the *Gates of Pearls*; commitment however, gets us there, not just good intensions. In the days ahead, many Christians will turn away because of the pressure the world's systems will exert on us. We must commit to following Christ now, so adversity wouldn't cause us to change our minds then.

Job's story shows that sometimes, God uses adversity to teach us or to build our faith. We should always do our best to overcome adversity, but when we realize that the adversity we are encountering is a teaching lesson from God, we should submit to it.

Ruth's story illustrates this principle. Ruth ran into devastating circumstances. All Ruth had in her life were dead men: A dead husband, a dead brother-in-law and a dead father-in-law, but Ruth submitted to this adversity. Even when her mother-in-law encouraged her to leave she refused to go.

> But Ruth said:
> *"Entreat me not to leave you, or to turn back from following after you; For wherever you go, I will go; And wherever you lodge, I will lodge; Your people shall be my people, And your God, my God. Where you die, I will die, And there will I be buried. The Lord do so to me, and more also, If anything but death parts you and me."*
> **– Ruth 1:16-17** *(NKJV)*

Orpah took the easy way, but Ruth submitted to adversity and it paid off. If you check the genealogy of Jesus in **Matthew 1,** you'll see Ruth's name among all those men.

Repentance

Submission and repentance go together. Repentance for sin demonstrates submission to Christ. The Greek work for repentance is **metaneo** which means *change of one's mind.* A biblical definition then would be to feel truly remorseful over one's sins. To repent, therefore, means to acknowledge one's sinfulness, be sincerely remorseful and to humble oneself before God. Repentance is not just a verbal expression; it involves confessing and turning away from a known sinful behavior.

Especially among today's political correctness and humanistic cultures, the subject of sin makes people feel uncomfortable,

but this discomfort is a necessary aspect of salvation's process. *Holy Spirit* challenges us to confront our sins and repent; otherwise, rebirth cannot take place. Christians who understand and teach this have been labeled as religious bigots or arrogant because we know that we cannot change the essence of the gospel's message. The Lord Himself handed the church's doctrine down to us and...

...Repentance is an essential prerequisite for sins to be forgiven.

John the Baptist's message was, *"Repent for the kingdom of heaven is at hand."* This stark, succinct doctrine had never been preached before John. In fact, between **Malachi** and **Matthew** it appears that heaven was silent for over four hundred years. History of God working in Israel is silent and it appears that there was no revelation or no one heard from God during that time. Then John came preaching a message of repentance. But John was only the forerunner - the one sent to introduce Jesus. Even before Herod beheaded John, Jesus; *the Son of Almighty God, the Savior of the world*, the one who paved the way for man's redemption, picked up from where John left off and preached the same message:

> *"From that time, Jesus began to preach, and to say, Repent: for the kingdom of heaven is at hand."*
>
> – **Matthew 4:17**

In **Luke 24:47** He instructed:

> *"That repentance and remission of sins should be preached in his name among all nations, beginning at Jerusalem."*

Is there a need for Christians to repent? Absolutely! **John 9:41** and **1 John 1:8** speaks of this, *"If we say that we have no sin, we deceive ourselves, and the truth is not in us."* Even after we have repented of our sins and have been regenerated, we commit sins by omission or by commission. We should repent of them as Holy Spirit makes us aware of them. I'm sure you'll admit that He is daily opening our eyes to things we did that we were not aware that they were sins. Are there any sins He's been addressing and you have been trying to avoid? No? How about dishonoring the Sabbath by shopping on Sundays? How about not tithing?

Jesus lived in a very religious environment, but the scriptures make it clear which sins upset Him most – self righteousness – justifying oneself before God. Jesus said a person is defiled from within. Repentance therefore, is not just addressing outward sins, but inward sins as well. Repentance from outward sin is useless if internal sins are not dealt with as well. I may not get some of my Calvinist friends to agree with me, but regretfully, Christians who trivialize the importance of repentance after being saved, will not make it through the gates.

Repentance also covers a broader area than addressing personal sin. Many Christians today are seeing spiritual breakthroughs as they repent for the sins of our age. Daniel was a devout man, yet he spent time repenting for Israel's sins. We should follow his example, humble ourselves and repent for the sins of our family, our churches and our country as well.

> *"Even while I was praying and confessing my sin and the sins of my people, desperately pleading with the Lord my God for Jerusalem, His holy mountain."*
>
> **– Daniel 9:20** *(TLB)*

Humility

The mark of a true Christian is humility. You can always recognize someone who had a personal encounter with Jesus. There is a sense of humility in their character. Just like Isaiah when he saw God, they understand the need for repentance as a prerequisite for standing in God's presence. I saw a man on television who had an encounter with Jesus. Twenty years later and he was still in tears.

Humility is a key agent in a successful run to the Gates of Pearls. A very different scale measures success here. We measure success by one's accomplishments in life, but success from God's perspective centers on spiritual accolades instead of secular achievements. The little preacher that God called out of drug addiction and sent him to preach in a little store-front in an inner city, he understands humility.

- *If* he never gains more than ten members;
- *If* he doesn't always have heat in the church building;
- *If* he is never able to buy a nice suit or a dress for his wife;
- *If* he can never afford toys for his children at Christmas;
- *If* he dies of malnutrition and his family can't even afford a decent casket for him;
- *If* he endures to the end, **God considers him a success**.

This is not about a vow of poverty; this is about humility. This is about humbling ourselves before the Lord and doing God's will, even when earthly pleasures aren't available. Jesus showed us humility in coming to earth and submitting to the death of the cross.

Let's follow His example and humble ourselves before God in all that God asks of us. **1 Peter 5:6** says:

> *"Humble yourselves therefore under the mighty hand of God, that He may exalt you in due time."*

A Surrendered Life

Submission involves humility and surrender. Humility precedes a surrendered life. From the Christian's perspective, the two are inseparable criteria for entrance to heaven – not religion or denomination. It would be ludicrous for me to say that only Pentecostals will enter heaven. I do not have the audacity to speculate whether any particular denomination will cross the finish line. In fact, any denomination or religious faction that believes and preaches that they are the only ones who will cross heavens' finish line, they are blatantly lying. The Apostle John was transported into the future and saw,

> *"...a great multitude, which no man could number, of all nations, and kindreds, and people, and tongues, stood before the throne, and before the Lamb, clothed with white robes, and palms in their hands."*
> **– Revelation 7:9**

A robe washed in the blood of the Lamb is the deciding factor for entrance to heaven.

> *"... And he said to me, These are they which came out of great tribulation, and have washed their robes, and made them white in the blood of the Lamb."*
> **– Revelation 7:14**

A total surrender to Christ is critical for those who'll have their robes washed and will enter the *Gates of Pearls*. Sadly, not every Christian understands how important this is. The statistics of the parable of the Sower shows that only 25 percent of Christians who start on this journey mature enough to produce fruit. Only 1/4 of those who start out reach the finish line.

- Surrendering to Christ is critical for salvation.
- Surrendering is critical for sustenance and growth.
- Surrendering is critical for crossing the finish line.

It is important that we surrender to the Lord Jesus Christ when we hear His voice. I was appalled when I realized that people can sit under *"ultra holiness preaching and teaching"* and still not surrender to the Lord. Some people remain set in their ways regardless of how passionate the preacher preaches. They will not allow even the most anointed, Spirit led, revealed Word of God to change their mindset. Many of them are dedicated church members, but their hearts have grown so hard; Jesus Himself could come and preach, still, they wouldn't change. They don't understand the importance of surrendering to Christ.

"While it is said, today if ye will hear His voice, harden not your hearts, as in the provocation."

– Hebrews 3:15

A few years ago, a lady visited our church and said she was praying about an issue. In a dream, God told her, *"Go to Mount Carmel."* She visited other Mount Carmel churches, but was not convinced that any of them was the church God meant. In another dream, God told her *"Mount Carmel is a blue & white church."* She noticed our blue & white church one day and came the next

Sunday with a friend. God touched her friend so profoundly, they were both dumfounded. She shared her story of how God directed her to Mount Carmel, but stressed that she would not be giving up her *(J W)* religion. She visited quite often and even brought some of her family. As I taught on the importance of being rooted and grounded in the Word in order to withstand false religion, she was offended and left. How sad! God answered her prayers and showed her the way. She chose her way instead of surrendering to God's way.

Those who cross the finish line however, are different. They understand that Jesus surrendered even to the death of the cross and those who will follow Him must have the same mindset. They don't necessarily have to be in a spiritually charged environment to hear the Savior's voice. They hear His still, small voice; even through the feeble words of a baby Christian, and surrender to Him. They bow before Him in humble submission; they change their ways, they adjust their attitudes and repent when necessary. These surrendering Christians will certainly cross the finish line and join the elders and angels in heavenly worship.

Progression to Worship

Worship and submission are inseparable. Worship begins with the surrendering of our will to God. Jesus said in **John 4:24** –

> *"God is a Spirit: and they that worship Him must worship Him in spirit and in truth."*

The type of worship that God expects from us is therefore, the kind that is done in the spirit. We do not know *(naturally)* how to offer the right type of worship, but our spirit knows. God created

our spirit to communicate with Him, so our spirit knows how to worship God; our flesh does not! Since we live, communicate and interact in the flesh, there must therefore be a progression to worship. This progression starts in our minds as we first submit to the concept of worship, but it is not automatic.

After we submit to the concept of worship in our minds, we must then challenge our own fleshly abilities to follow the submission process. That is, we bring our organs, our muscular system and our five senses into subjection to the will of God. As we persevere *(in our flesh)* in subjecting our entire being to God's will, our spirit gains more control. As this process continues where our flesh becomes increasingly subjected to God's will, our spirit prevails even more. The more control our spirit has over our flesh, the more acceptable our worship becomes. This is, therefore, a progression of worship. We start to worship with our natural resources and abilities, and progress to worshiping God through our spirit. Submission is the catalyst that brings us into God's presence.

How To...

Submit to God. *This is essential for reaching the gates.*

Submit to Christ *now so you won't flinch when adversity arises.*

Reconcile *with your family, especially with your ex.*

Repent *of sins as Holy Spirit makes you aware of them.*

Repent *of the sins of our culture, our community and our country.*

Prioritize *seeing the Lord Jesus Christ at the Gates of Pearls.*

Stand firm *on your decision to follow Christ even through trials.*

Challenge *your fleshly abilities to follow the submission process of worship.*

MY PERSONAL THOUGHTS &
INSPIRATIONS

CHAPTER 3
DESTINY HINDRANCES

What is the criteria for entrance to heaven? Will following the principles of any religion get us there? Many religions tout their way there. Can all of us be correct? Does Christianity own the rights to the way to heaven? If Christianity offers the sole way, why can't we all *join together* since we are going to the same place? Why is there so much conflict in the church today?

Many things come to hinder us from reaching our destiny, but conflict in the Church is the most unsettling. The last place one should expect conflict is in the Church. Regretfully, conflict is a growing characteristic of today's Church. Conflict in the Church is frustrating especially to pastors because it antagonizes all that they preach to their congregations *Sunday after Sunday*. Some Christians thrive on conflict. To them, the Church is their private gossip club and they've been called and anointed by a higher power to keep some type of conflict active. They become restless if some drama is not going on.

Unfortunately, conflict in the Church is something today's Christian must learn to cope with because it is happening almost everywhere. I have been a pastor for over twenty years and it saddens me to think of the actions and habits of some Christians. After twenty years of pastoring I shouldn't be surprised, but I am appalled that even after sincere, energetic preaching, teaching and counseling, some Christians still instigate *bickering* and *conflict*. Some walk around with pride, bitterness, grudges and unforgiveness and yet believe that they are on their way to heaven. **Hebrews 12:15** challenges us to shun this behavior:

> *"Looking diligently lest any man fail of the grace of God; lest any root of bitterness springing up trouble you, and thereby many be defiled."*

See also **Galatians 5:20-21.**

When Christians act in unchristian-like ways it is not because they are just mean. They are just unhappy because they have lost their way. You need to understand this so you won't allow them to cause you to lose your directions as well. Seeing the *Gates of Pearls* is not on their destination list. In many cases, it is not even on their itinerary. They are on the highway because they have joined a church, but they are not committed to Christ, neither have they renewed their minds. Many of them are broken down vehicles, causing accidents, rubbernecking and even the death of other travelers. Don't let them prevent you from seeing the gates. It's okay to be selfish in this respect. Don't focus so much on the shortcomings of others. Concentrate on what you need to do to reach the gates. In **1 Corinthians 9:27**, Paul wrote:

> *"But I keep under my body, and bring it into subjection: lest that by any means, when I have preached to others, I myself should be a castaway."*

Where It Originates

All conflict originates in the spirit realm, so we cannot go much farther on our journey before addressing the effect that the spirit realm has on the actions, reactions and mindset of people here

on earth, including Christians. I must admit that although I was born and raised in the Church, I was naïve about this subject until God taught me about it after a few sad experiences.

Conflicts stem from evil principalities and powers operating in our atmosphere

As noted in **2 Corinthians 4:4** and **Ephesians 6:12**, *principalities* and *powers* in the atmosphere instigate conflict. These evil forces manipulate people's minds and block their vision so they cannot comprehend the principles of *God's word*. These evil atmospheric spirits are *devious* and *deceptive*. They affect every facet of our spiritual, social, and economic well-being. Some Christians are not aware of the evil, destructive schemes of these forces.

> *"And no wonder, for Satan himself masquerades as an angel of light."*
> – **2 Corinthians 11:14** *(NIV)*

In times of spiritual revival, we experience less resistance from our adversaries, but we can all agree that we are losing many battles today. The forces of darkness are not just attacking the Church; they are invading and occupying even the pulpit. Much of the modern Church is not aware of this subtle invasion.

In January 2005, God showed me that some Christians entertain evil spirits and are not aware that they entertain them. A list of these evil spirits that Christians entertain include spirits of envy, spirits of pride, spirits of complacency, spirits of strife, lying spirits, spirits of jealousy, spirits of self-righteousness, and many others. The Lord told me that every Christian is responsible for exercising the authority Jesus gave us and to command all evil spirits to vacate our surroundings. He said that although I was the pastor and had authority over demons, there was little I could do to help them since they allowed the evil spirit to stay and inadvertently manipulate their minds.

Evil spirits are deceptive.

That's why we may not know when we are entertaining them. If we entertain one *(like pride)* it will keep the door of our mind ajar so others can enter. Since they are all deceptive, they will manipulate our minds and we wouldn't see anything wrong with our actions.

> *"If the Good News we preach is hidden to anyone, it is hidden from the one who is on the road to eternal death. **Satan, who is the god of this evil world, has made him blind, unable to see the glorious light of the Gospel that is shining upon him** or to understand the amazing message we preach about the glory of Christ, who is God."*

– **2 Corinthians 4:3-4** *(TLB)* emphasis is mine

As a pastor, I have seen many members under this yoke. It hurts to know that they need deliverance and they don't know that they need it. If their minds are open I can help them, but they are usually resistant to instructions and they see things from a different perspective. They will argue and misinterpret all that God inspires me to do. Even if I use fifty different illustrations from various angles to explain an issue, the evil spirit they are entertaining will turn things around so they will interpret my instructions very differently. Unless they are open to God's directives, the evil spirit will continue to manipulate and deceive them. These spirits resist the Word of God and especially the gifts of the Spirit. Rather than repenting and turning away from wrong when the word of knowledge operates, these manipulated Christians will resent the word of knowledge and often accuse the person *(who ministered the word)* of meddling in their business.

Manipulative spirits seek to control others

Evil spirits are invisible but we recognize their presence by the attitudes and actions of the people they influence. In **Revelation 2:20**, *Jesus* said *Thyatira* was guilty of allowing *Jezebel* to teach and lead His people astray. Jezebel was dead hundreds of years before, so what could Jesus be referring to? Jesus meant the Jezebel spirit not Jezebel the person. This spirit is a manipulative spirit that seeks to control others. It challenges authority and often seeks to promote its own agenda by cunningly tearing down established principles and leadership. Jezebel is dead indeed, but the spirit that bears her name is *(sadly)* still alive and operating in many places today.

With *Holy Spirit's* help, you will recognize deceptive spirits and counteract their agenda in your life - even in your Church. Don't overstep your pastor's authority, but you don't have to wait for him or her to deal with the various spirits that some Christians entertain. The pastor may be the object of their attack. **Luke 10:19** did not say that power and authority was given only to church leaders. You! Yes! You have the authority to bind evil spirits and bar them from operating in your life and in your Church. If you use your authority and command them to leave, you will see more peace and less conflict in your surroundings. Jesus gave you authority over all evil spirits. He placed this book in your hands to remind you that He did, so use the authority He gave you.

"Behold, I give unto you power to tread on serpents and scorpions, and over all the power of the enemy: and nothing shall by any means hurt you."

– Luke 10:19

The spirit realm far exceeds even human comprehension, yet it exists around us at all times. It is not wise to bury our head in the sand, hoping that these things aren't so. The bride of Christ must understand that we are engaged in an ongoing spiritual war against these forces. What transpires in the spirit realm affects the way we live, the way we react and our eternal destiny as well. The Church alone offers resistance to the operation of evil forces in the atmosphere. That is why there is so much conflict in the Church. The forces of darkness are trying to divide us. Understand that we must fight against them.

Have you ever wondered why Paul used the illustration of wrestling and fighting to describe the Christians' walk? To get to the gates we have to wrestle *(fight, struggle)* with these forces of darkness. Christians are not exempted from this atmospheric influence. In fact, Christians are more impacted by the spirit realm than non Christians. On one side, angels are fighting on our behalf while on the other side evil spirits are trying to kill, destroy and divert us.

Although this spirit realm impacts us, we still determine our destiny. We determine whether we see the *Gates of Pearls*, not only because Jesus defeated all our opposition, but He gave us His victory belt. We have authority over all the forces of darkness. Although there are many of these evil spirits around us, they are not enough of them to prevent us from reaching the *Gates of Pearls*.

"And Jesus came and spake unto them, saying, All power is given unto me in heaven and in earth."

– **Matthew 28:18**

But evil spirits are a menace. They make the journey from here to the *Gates of Pearls* a treacherous path. They lay traps for us and dig huge potholes along the highway and ambush Christians, especially in lonely places. They shoot at us and *throw stones* from all angles. They are determined to deceive us, distract us, divert us or discourage us in any way or by any means possible. They work tirelessly studying our lifestyle to find all our vulnerabilities. So, in the Church our enemy manipulates Christians and uses them to divert other Christians from the path to glory. He knows that a divided kingdom cannot stand, so he divides us in an effort to defeat us.

Self Evaluation

This brings us to a critical junction where we need to be honest and sincere about doing whatever it takes to make it to the gates. How would we know if we are entertaining one of these spirits? Most likely, we wouldn't know. We know when we have the *fruits of the Spirit*, but we may not be aware that we are *mean* and *selfish* or that we are *entertaining a spirit of Jezebel*. God has to show us these personality flaws in us and then we must be willing to change when He does.

Are you willing to be transparent?

Do you know some pleasant, loving, generous Christians? They know that they are pleasant individuals. Do you know any mean, grumpy and selfish Christians? They don't know they are mean, grumpy and selfish. To them, that's the way they see the world. To them, you have a problem; not them. If this is your personality type you wouldn't know it either, but you can change to a loving, generous, pleasant personality. Self can be the greatest hindrance to our destiny. Are you willing to be transparent? Don't trust your own perception. It is critical that you ask *Holy Spirit* to turn the spotlight on you. You must allow Him to search your heart and show you the issues He finds. Then you must make the necessary changes.

> *"Search me, O God, and know my heart: try me, and know my thoughts."* — **Psalms 139:23**

Some individuals have grown up in an abusive home. That environment created and shaped a bitter, resentful personality in them. Although they have embraced Christianity, testify of being saved and even filled with the *Holy Spirit*, they are still bitter and resentful. They exemplify this in their interaction even with other church members. Some of them could have enjoyed a good marriage, but their bitter personality suffocated and killed their marriage relationship. They'll be quick to tell you of all the ills and shortcomings of their spouse, yet their spouse could be the best thing that ever happened to them. *Their bitterness - the mote in their eyes, blinded them to their own shortcomings.*

These individuals usually have an egotistical personality and no counseling, regardless of how passionate, spiritual, and sincere can change their mindset. God and God alone can help these individuals and even then, they will have to be open to His succinct, sharp correction if they are to realize pertinent change.

Indeed, the environment where they were raised impacted and shaped their personality. A negative force overpowered them.

They were vulnerable, weak and not able to resist the individuals who created the hostile environment. Change, even spiritual, is an uphill battle for them. Often, the requirements for change challenges them to dismantle the psychological walls they've built to protect them from further abuse. The same walls however, can prevent them from making it to the *Gates of Pearls*. They'll need a miracle if they are to reach the gates. And yes; God is still performing miracles.

Look over the characteristics I have just described. How does your demeanor compare with any of them? Be honest! Don't forget you are on the road to heaven. If this description fits you, as harsh and as painful as it may be, you must face this issue and modify your conduct before trying to proceed any further. Although the environment shaped you, you are the only one who can correct your situation. The choice is yours. You can put this book down and believe that God will overlook your posture, or you can deal with the issue right now. You are blessed beyond measure however, to have *Holy Spirit* reach behind your wall and speak to your heart through the pages of this book, but you have to trust Him!

- Slowly drop your defense and lay vulnerable before Him.
- **Trust Him!** – To help you stand even if you fall flat on your face initially.
- **Trust Him!** – To help you struggle through possible humiliation or even ridicule.
- **Trust Him!** – Even if wounds you thought were healed, reopen and fresh, hot blood rushes out again.

Removing the hindrance of self may be difficult but you must do it. If you continue to depend on the wall you've created, you won't experience God's peace. You won't find out how *Holy Spirit* speaks in a still, small voice to sooth inner pain and restlessness. A happy social relationship may not find you either, even after the second or third marriage. Please dismantle your wall and lean solely on God for protection. Take an extended look in the mirror. The problem is not as much in others as it is in the person you see there. Your wall of defense has actually become a wall of offence. You are the problem and you need to know it. When you stand before God He is going to question you about how you treated others, not necessarily about how others treated you. You offend others more than you encourage them. *Drop your egotism. Drop your self-centeredness. Discard your pride and ask Holy Spirit to help you knock down the wall you have built around you.*

- **Ask Him** to open your eyes so you won't offend people.

- **Ask Him** to help you to forgive those who did you wrong.

- **Ask Him** to help you make it to the *Gates of Pearls*.

Heaven is our destination.

God wants us to be with Him in heaven. Jesus wants us there as well, so we must be wise to utilize all the tools to dismantle all destiny hindrances. Our enemy is cunning but some Christians are too slick for his game. They see him coming from far away and they always defeat him. They stay prayed up! They study God's word and allow it to abide in them. They are resistant fireballs against all the fiery darts of the wicked. After storms, after trials and after great battles, they are left still standing. It doesn't even matter if they don't have money in their pocket, clothes on their backs or enough food on their table; they are trouble for Satan's camp. He doesn't have enough artillery to keep them from consistently popping their heads back up and firing back at him. So, reluctantly, he pulls out his last arsenal – ***persecution.***

Persecution

Persecution shows that our adversary is desperate. His intent is to use persecution as a hindrance. Over the years however, this arsenal has actually united Christians and made them more resilient. Church history shows that during periods of persecution, Christianity realized its highest levels of piety and expansion. Millions of Christians have been martyred since Jesus established the Church, but the Church survived. Many Christians have been tortured in countries of the former Soviet Union, but today both religious and physical walls have been torn down and the church's light has rekindled there. A communist regime still governs China today and Chinese Christians are experiencing grave persecution, imprisonment and even death, yet Christians there are more ardent and charismatic than Christians in the Western world. Persecution has done much good for the Church. We should learn from history then and not be so anxious to relish an end to persecution. Chinese Christians understand this. While we are praying that persecution would end there, some Chinese Christians are praying that persecution would come to America. They know the power of a persecuted Church and they see the lethargy of a worry free, lax, Western Church.

History shows that the edict that ended persecution and propelled Christianity to a prominent position in the great *Roman Empire* was not a significant accomplishment for Christianity at all. Political and social acceptance of its practices proved to be a most devastating blow to the Christian ideology. In fact, looking in retrospect, we can see that the whole episode *(the apparent victory)* was a devious scheme by Satan to sidetrack the Church which until then had proven to be an expanding, formidable foe: strong and unbreakable. After persecution ended, the Church grew slack and uncommitted until it became dormant for over one thousand years. We should be cautious then, about the strategy of religious freedom that our adversary is using against the Church.

Overcomer

Persecution, discomforts and various challenges will come to hinder us as we seek the *Gates of Pearls*. In spite of this, many have already overcome. Someone today will overcome every trial, every heartache and every obstacle that is placed in our path and make a successful run to the *Gates of Pearls*. Amidst the challenges, pitfalls and hindrances you can also be one of those who persevere and succeed.

If you persist, I envision that you wouldn't even have to knock at the gate when you get there. Angels will see you when you turn the last corner towards home. Shouts of applause and welcome will erupt from the crowds of already successful runners who are standing there to greet victorious Christians.

Maybe the old mothers from your Church are there anxiously waiting to see if anyone from their Church will be the next one to turn the corner. But it will be you. Yes you! As the bright lights of the city pierces through the golden gates *(which will be in your view),* you'll walk the last mile-stretch with dignity and gratitude. Demons will then retreat in defeat, confessing that they did all they could to stop you, but you overcame by the *blood of the Lamb* and the *word of your testimony*. With a pleasurable smirk, angels who fought for you will tap you on the shoulder and tell you *"Go on in now"* as they turn back to assist others who are still on the rugged pathway.

Until the last blood washed believer makes it to the gate, angels will not give up. They cannot take for granted that the battle is over. Somewhere, back on the highway, a believer is about to give up because they've been in a violent valley for a long, long time. Demons have kept the pressure on them and are smelling success. They are sure this believer will surrender soon, so they've called in reinforcements to secure their victory. But angels hastily return from ensuring your successful entrance, to engage in the struggle – if only to whisper in the believer's ear:

*"Hold on. You can make it.
Jesus is only a prayer away!"*

"Fear none of those things which thou shalt suffer: behold, the devil shall cast some of you into prison, that ye may be tried; and ye shall have tribulation ten days: be thou faithful unto death, and I will give thee a crown of life."
— **Revelation 2:10**

How To...

All destiny hindrances originate in the spirit realm. These evil forces are attacking our finances, our health, our marriage, our children and anything we have that's valuable. Understand that you have to fight against them if you are to overcome all hindrances to your destiny.

- Fight, using every weapon that God has given you.
- Exercise your faith and fight.

- Use your speech to negate what your senses detect.
- Pray more than you have ever prayed before.
- Fast more often than you have ever fasted before.
- Don't ever stop going to church. Even if all hell breaks loose at the Church, don't leave unless God tells you to leave. Don't try to coerce God into sanctioning your leaving either.
- Read God's word. Open your heart to *Holy Spirit* and allow Him to direct *(or re-direct)* your footsteps.

"Wherefore take unto you the whole armour of God, that ye may be able to withstand in the evil day, and having done all, to stand."

– Ephesians 6:13

Put on the whole armor of God to overcome all destiny hindrances. God, Jesus, Holy Spirit or angels will not put on this armor and fight for you. You must put on this armor and fight for yourself; then, they will help you.

"Put on the strong belt of truth and the breastplate of God's approval.
Wear shoes that are able to speed you on as you preach the Good News of peace with God.
In every battle, you will need faith as your shield to stop the fiery arrows aimed at you by Satan.
And you will need the helmet of salvation and the sword of the Spirit-which is the Word of God.
Pray all the time. Ask God for anything in line

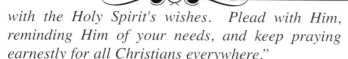

with the Holy Spirit's wishes. Plead with Him, reminding Him of your needs, and keep praying earnestly for all Christians everywhere."

– **Ephesians 6:14-18** *(TLB)*

The devil can only defeat you if you let him. Don't ever stop fighting against him.

Fight until you cross the finish line.

Fight and succeed so you can truly identify with *Apostle Paul:*

"I have fought a good fight, I have finished my course, and I have kept the faith."
– **2 Timothy 4:7**

- Success is not measured by how many accolades people or institutions place on our shoulders.
- It is not how well we can preach, teach or pray.
- It is not even the amount of wealth we accumulate.

Success is crossing the threshold of heaven's gate, the final laying down of our armor at the feet of Jesus and hearing Him say to us, *"Well Done - You have overcome all destiny hindrances."*

MY PERSONAL THOUGHTS & INSPIRATIONS

CHAPTER 4
HopE

If this book finds you at a low point in your journey, please recluse from thoughts of giving up, refocus on your destination and keep your eyes on the prize there. Relax and allow me also to speak into your life. It will do you much good if you would just sit still and listen carefully to what I'll be saying in this chapter. You are going through a bleak valley. I understand your predicament, but I refuse to join you on your seat of despondency. Too many Christians lose hope in this valley. Friends abandon friends here as the sign just up ahead entices them to take a less wearisome route. Any other route however, is not trustworthy, so you must travel through this valley. Big and bold as it appears, the sign up ahead that invites travelers to exit the next two miles is not for you. The amenities it is offering are appealing indeed! Whoever created this sign, obviously knows the dreariness of this valley and the consequent mindset of the travelers.

- *They* have researched your personality.
- *They* know your cravings and your tendencies.
- *They* have captured some of your prayers.
- *They* know what you've been crying to God about.
- *They* have intercepted many of the answers.
- *They* know you are overwhelmed.

So, the billboard advertises all the amenities your body and spirit desires: rest, relaxation, food, friendship, but this is not your exit. Bright lights are on the sign and the area seems well lit, but this is not your exit. I admit its advertisements are enticing; even more so as you grapple with the surrounding conditions. Darkness and danger however, looms for those who take this exit. You may be at your lowest low, but don't be deceived by this false advertising. Don't take this exit. You may not get back on the highway. If you exit at this time, you could possibly lose your life.

Discouragement County

Discouragement County is almost at the end of this gloomy valley. Is discouragement legitimate? You have come a long way; you have been through many difficult valleys, yet you don't see a trail of success to merit continuing. Disappointment has been a faithful, but nagging associate in almost all of your efforts. Every inner evaluation suggests that you should be discouraged. You've tried and you have failed. You've tried and you have failed. You've tried and you have failed. Your heart is breaking and you are exhausted because fulfillment of your dreams has consistently evaded you. Often, you ask yourself, *"Does it really make any sense to try anymore?"* Faith and patience, however, are virtues that even the devil cannot outrun.

I must tell you some things about *Discouragement County*. The weather conditions here are poor, but you must not allow them to affect you. Also, the devil attacks our minds violently in this county, so you must decide not to be mentally frustrated either. Although the disparaging conditions seem to justify a "what's the use" demeanor, and although the Lord Jesus weeps for you as you struggle in this area, you must pull yourself out. You must get out of this county immediately. You must not entertain anything that delays you in this valley.

Galatians 6:9 *(TLB)* says:

> *"And let us not get tired of doing what is right, for after a while we will reap a harvest of blessing if we don't get discouraged and give up."*

If we get discouraged and give up, we won't reap a harvest. Discouragement is not an attribute of heaven. It does not originate there. Although the surrounding conditions dictate that you should be disheartened, entertaining discouragement constitutes a sin. I know the situation looks grim. All your past efforts may be filled with disappointment, but to entertain discouragement is to side with the devil. It is to walk in unbelief. Like Israel in the wilderness, many Christians walk around in circles in this discouragement county and never get back on the highway.

> *"Therefore, my beloved brethren, be ye steadfast, unmovable, always abounding in the work of the Lord, forasmuch as ye know that your labor is not in vain in the Lord."*
> **– 1 Corinthians 15:58**

I command you to get out of this valley now! The devil is a liar. Discouragement is not legitimate. It is not justifiable! Ask *Holy Spirit* to take away all the hurt, the pain of disappointment and to help you overcome discouragement. I assure you that He will do that for you. He will take it away so far from you that even if you want to be discouraged you won't be able find it.

God Cares

God cares about us enough to make provision for us so we wouldn't fall into the deceptive traps of the enemy in this valley.

- How can we know that God cares about us when we are at our lowest low?
- What assures us that He cares when we are so broke even poor folk call us poor?
- Where is God when we are so distraught that we wish a hole would open in the ground and swallow us?
- Why does it seem like the whole world is enjoying life while we keep getting a raw deal?

Sometimes you may question whether the Christian life is even worth living. Let me assure you however, that God cares about you-especially during those times. You may think that no one cares about you, but let me assure you that as long as you have started on the road to the *Gates of Pearls*, you are blessed and highly favored. It may not seem that way sometimes, but you have all the resources of heaven supporting you.

Circumstances can overwhelm you and tears may be your constant companion. Tears will blur your natural vision, but they can also serve as telescopes through which you see far beyond your present circumstances. Your night may seem long, but I speak to you with profound assurance that you don't have to fail in this valley. On your own two feet, you can walk this street to glory. As long as you keep walking you will survive all the storms. Jesus said He would never leave us or forsake us, so He is right there with you even though you don't feel, see or hear Him.

God, Jesus and all of heaven are more concerned about you than you think. Yes! You are in a deep, deep valley and heaven is in silence, not because of shock or lack of resources. Heaven is in quiet suspense, anxiously awaiting your next move. Celestial and terrestrial eyes are on you because *(like Job)* the Father has boasted about you. He boasted: *"You will not shrink or surrender to*

Satan's onslaught. You will succeed." So, tension is thick! Will God's team win again? Will they applaud in jubilation as you stubbornly remain standing or just keep getting back up? Will you give up? In your mind, that seems like the most obvious thing to do. Your hands and feet are sore, bloodied and scarred from tireless struggles, but just get up and walk beside me up this next hill. You will almost hear heaven's thunderous applause when you get back up. You may even sense the smile on Jesus' face as He turns to Father and says: *"Another victory for one whom I have washed in my blood."* Bless God! Bless God! That's you! Jesus is talking about you.

Keep Hope Alive

> *"Why art thou cast down, O my soul? and why art thou disquieted in me? Hope thou in God: for I shall yet praise Him for the help of His countenance."*
>
> **– Psalms 42:5**

Knowing that heaven is aware of every dilemma you face is encouraging, so keep hope alive. God will not allow more on you than you can bear. If everything you have tried to hold onto slips through your fingers, make sure you hold on to hope.

- Hope shakes stagnation out of the mind, rejects despair and always anticipates good.
- Hope breathes desire and always sees happiness even in the face of overwhelming sorrow.
- Hope is the foundation upon which certain, eventual success rests.
- Hope triumphs over all trials, difficulties and adversity.

- Hope is medicine for the sick, freedom for the prisoner and wealth to the poor.
- Hope reminds us that *"weeping may endure for a night but joy comes in the morning."* – **Psalms 30:5**
- Hope sings always in a quiet undertone that it is better farther on.
- Hope reassures us that heaven is real, that God is there and that He cares about us.

I reiterate that God cares about you! God notices the smallest details of your life. Our postmodern culture is saturated with greed, but God so loved that He gave. He gave because He loved! God cares so much about you that He gave His only Son to die on your behalf. He did this unconditionally. That means whether or not you would ever accept salvation, God went ahead and sacrificed His Son's life for you, anyway.

- God cares about you in every situation that troubles you.
- God cares about you when sickness knocks on your door.
- God cares about you when you lose a loved one.
- God cares about you when you lose your job or your business fails. So, hope in God.

Creating A Positive Attitude

Along this journey, you'll meet many people and you will make many friends. Some friends will stand with you no matter what you go through. Some friends will stay for a while, and then gradually leave. Sadly, some will forsake you when you need them most. It is especially during those times that you must not entertain despondency, but just keep moving forward.

> *"For in thee, O Lord, do I hope: thou wilt hear, O Lord my God."*
> — **Psalms 38:15**

Depression is not just a disposition; depression is the work of an evil spirit. As with any other evil spirit, you do not have to entertain depression in any of your surroundings. Whenever depression knocks at your door, create a positive attitude all around you by taking control of your emotions and telling yourself that you are not going to worry about the negative things in your life. You do not always have the luxury of the church setting or a Christian brother around to encourage you. The devil also takes advantage of those times of loneliness and isolation and uses them to discourage us. Don't wait until you get to church. Defeat him by creating a positive attitude. The Lord Jesus told us not to worry even when adversity overtakes us:

> *"What is the price of five sparrows? A couple of pennies? Not much more than that. Yet, God does not forget a single one of them. And He knows the number of hairs on your head!* ***Never fear, you are far more valuable to Him than a whole flock of sparrows****."*
> — **Luke 12:6-7** *(TLB)* emphasis is mine

God takes care of the little sparrows. There is never a shortage of worms to feed them. Are you convinced that you are worth more than a whole flock of sparrows? Note also that God takes the time to keep count of the hairs on your head? Wow! Why would God take the time to do that if He didn't care much about you? So whatever life throws your way, create a positive attitude. Life is not a bed of roses, and even if it were, even a beautiful, tender rose

grows on a stem that has sharp thorns. Why should I expect to have a problem free life while other Christians have endured and are enduring significant trials and suffering? That wouldn't be fair, would it? In **2 Timothy 3:12,** Paul said:

"All that will live godly in Christ Jesus shall suffer persecution."

In **1 Corinthians 4:11-13**, He gives a vivid picture of his own struggles: *NLT*

"Even now we go hungry and thirsty, and we don't have enough clothes to keep warm. We are often beaten and have no home. We work wearily with our own hands to earn our living. We bless those who curse us. We are patient with those who abuse us. We appeal gently when evil things are said about us. Yet we are treated like the world's garbage, like everybody's trash-right up to the present moment."

In spite of the many difficulties Paul faced, he turned out to be the greatest evangelist of his day and to the Church. Even with all his discomfort and trials Paul concluded in **Romans 8:37-39**:

"Nay, in all these things we are more than conquerors through him that loved us. For I am persuaded, that neither death, nor life, nor angels, nor principalities, nor powers, nor things present, nor things to come, nor height, nor depth, nor any other creature, shall be able to separate us from the love of God, which is in Christ Jesus our Lord."

So, don't just sit there feeling sorry for yourself and nursing discouragement because a friend forsook you when you needed them most. Grasp the same mindset. Many times, I've had to encourage others while I needed a good dose of encouragement myself. Categorically therefore, even when you don't sense God's presence or His awareness of your dire need, still hope! Even in your lowest, deepest or darkest valley, hold on to God's promises. Hope helps you to peer through an opening in heaven and confirm that God is still seated on the throne. God still sees our tomorrows even from yesterday and the sunshine that will come after the rain.

> *"But if we hope for that we see not, then do we with patience wait for it."*
>
> **– Romans 8:25**

Hebrews 10:35 says:

> *"Cast not away therefore your confidence, which hath great recompence of reward."*

We must journey in hope. We cannot see the gates from our location, but be assured that they have not moved. By mans' measurement, they are not a specific distance away, but they are there! Some people have been snatched away to them from your location. Others are still on the road behind you and some are up ahead. Hope alone is keeping many of them alert and committed. If you keep walking, you'll reach the gates in God's appointed time. If everything around you fails, make sure that you never lose hope.

> *"But let us, who are of the day, be sober, putting on the breastplate of faith and love; and for an helmet, **the hope of salvation**."*
>
> **– 1 Thessalonians 5:8** emphasis is mine

Prophesy in Hope

While you are walking through this valley, be careful what you say! You can negate hope by the words you say. Travelers on this road have been given vocal authority and that includes you. The words you speak express the nature of your heart. Your words can impact your spiritual wellbeing and determine your destination. Words have energy, so your words are prophetic. **Proverbs 18:21** says:

"Death and life is in the power of the tongue."

I met a woman who had inherited familiar spirits which she detested. I invited her to my church, but she just could not get there. Every Sunday morning something catastrophic would happen in her family that would prevent her from coming. I asked her: *"Are you saying that you are coming to my church?"* After she affirmed, I explained to her that God our Father knows everything, even our thoughts, but the devil and his demons do not know everything, so they do not know our thoughts. They know our plans as soon as we vocalize them, so they create situations to thwart them. I told her not to say that she would be coming to my church. She made it there. When you speak you prophesy; you change the course of history by your words.

Some Christians deviated from the path to glory because of the negative things they said about themselves. The negative words formed a reality that convinced them they could not continue. Your situation may look bleak, but always hope! Some people who stood in hope have even realized physical healing by speaking the Word of God instead of confessing their physician's diagnosis. So refrain from speaking negative things. Train your lips to speak positive things about yourself and about others around you. Prophesy to yourself and to your family that you are the head and not the tail – **Deuteronomy 28:5**. Especially while you are going through this dark valley, prophesy that one day you will lift up your right foot and put it over the threshold of the *Gates of Pearls*. Prophesy! Prophesy in hope.

One lady's family was in a car accident and her twelve year old son suffered terrible head injuries. She said that she put her hands into his brain at the accident site. The paramedics told her to say goodbye because they were sure he would not survive the trip to the hospital. Both parents said their goodbyes and the paramedics placed a white sheet over him. Then, a man showed up, pulled the sheet off and shouted: *"I speak life into you."* He also said, *"Satan, you will not have this kid's life tonight."* After months in the hospital, the doctors gave up on him. When his mother brought him home from the hospital, he was blind and deaf. He could not walk or talk and his entire body was in stricture. Ten years later and after numerous operations he is alive and doing everything medical science said he would not do. Someone spoke positive things over him. All through his ordeal, this lady spoke positive things from God's word over him.

Understand the power of the tongue. Hope gives you strength to speak against all the negative things that blare you in the face. Don't listen to negative things – not even in the hospital room. Even if you don't hear negative things or if you are not aware that they were spoken about you, they can still affect you since words have energy. Many people have terminated their journey and got off this road because of the negative things people spoke about them. Some have even experienced sickness and premature death because of this as well. Begin to override negative energy by speaking the Word of God repeatedly over yourself. Prophesy to your spirit:

"I can do all things through Christ which strengtheneth me."

– Phillippians 4:1

Prophesy In Hope

How To...

- Always remember that hope is medicine for the sick, freedom for the prisoner and wealth to the poor.
- Shake stagnation out of your mind by vocally rejecting despair.
- Triumph over difficulty and adversity through hope.
- Hope; even in the face of overwhelming sorrow.
- Break off any relationship with discouragement.
- Always remind yourself that *"weeping may endure for a night but joy comes in the morning."* **– Psalms 30:5**
- Remember that words have energy, so refrain from speaking negative things and practice speaking positive things in every situation.

Even if all your friends forsake you, keep moving forward. Don't ever give up. Even if you have one foot in the grave, keep hope alive! If you must go, go in hope, but until your last breath, let the devil know that you are not going out without hope.
Create a positive attitude and change the atmosphere around you by quoting these hope scriptures: ***Emphasis is all mine***.

> *"For we are saved by **hope**: but hope that is seen is not hope: for what a man seeth, why doth he yet hope for?"*

– Romans 8:24

*"And **hope** maketh not ashamed; because the love of God is shed abroad in our hearts by the Holy Ghost which is given unto us."*

– **Romans 5:5**

*"Which **hope** we have as an anchor of the soul, both sure and stedfast, and which entereth into that within the veil."*

– **Hebrews 6:19**

*"Who against **hope** believed in **hope**, that he might become the father of many nations, according to that which was spoken, So shall thy seed be."*

– **Romans 4:18**

*"For the **hope** which is laid up for you in heaven, whereof ye heard before in the word of the truth of the gospel."*

– **Colossians 1:5**

*"Looking for that blessed **hope**, and the glorious appearing of the great God and our Saviour Jesus Christ."*

– **Titus 2:13**

*"The eyes of your understanding being enlightened; that ye may know what is the **hope** of His calling, and what the riches of the glory of his inheritance in the saints."*

– **Ephesians 1:18**

God bless you!

MY PERSONAL THOUGHTS & INSPIRATIONS

CHAPTER 5
DOORWAYS TO THE SOUL

In **Proverbs 4:23**, *Solomon*, the wisest man that ever lived said, *"Guard your heart above all else, for it determines the course of your life" (NLT)*. Even after we are saved we need to guard our hearts like a lion guards her cubs. Very often, the Bible refers to the heart of man and the soul as the same. The soul consists of our five senses, the seat of our emotions-–the real you! As Solomon suggests, there are various doorways to our soul which we need to guard to prevent unwelcome influences.

- *We* must be vigilant.
- *We* must never let our guard down.
- *We* must be keen on the sneaky ways of our enemy.

1 Peter 5:8 advises us to:

> *"Be sober, be vigilant; because your adversary the devil, as a roaring lion, walketh about, seeking whom he may devour."*

Job's story illustrates that the devil was doing the same thing back then: *"Walking about, seeking whom he may devour."* He is doing the same thing today also, but he can only devour if we allow him to enter any of the doorways to our soul. We must repeatedly remind ourselves that we are in a spiritual war; otherwise, we'll grow negligent and drop our guard. This would be an unfortunate and costly mistake. God's word says:

"My people are destroyed for lack of knowledge."
– Hosea 4:6

What we don't know can hurt us. God is revealing much information to the body of Christ in these last days, but we are responsible for grasping all we can to help us in the fight against our enemy. When people stand before God to be judged for their life's activities, *"I didn't know"* is not going to be an acceptable excuse. It would be preposterous for us to reject the things *Holy Spirit* is revealing to the Church and yet expect to walk through the gates of the holy city.

Some things we consider as petty, yet they are devastating to our spiritual wellbeing. Some cultural associations, celebrations, festivals and various types of entertainment fall into this category. We may not be aware of them, but they may even prevent us from entering the holy city. Sometimes the seemingly trifling things are *"open doorways to the soul."* If we are not aware of these doorways to our soul, many of them will be open to our enemy. You may open some of them inadvertently. Others, you'll open presumptuously, while others may *(unknowingly)* be pried open by our adversary. This prying could be by someone or something used by him. The following lists some of the doorways of the soul. As I expose them, be prepared to close any you have open to our adversary and deny him access.

Doorways

Rejection – Some adopted kids face rejection. They cry silently because something is consistently whispering in their ears

that their parents didn't want them and no one else wants them either. Even when some of these children are adopted by loving, peaceful and sociable or well off parents, lying whisperers *(spirits)* are able to control their minds and steal their happiness.

Many children also face rejection among social groups in schools. School is a harsh place for many these days. Because of rejection by various groups, some children withdraw into seclusion until they lash out. Often, people who had nothing to do with their rejection get caught in the crossfire.

Almost everyone struggles with some form of rejection.

Divorcees for example – The spouse that walked out of the marriage may not necessarily be affected in this area, but the one who gave their marriage their best shot, only to have their partner run off with another person; this rejection creates a huge doorway. If you are in this situation you must not allow thoughts of rejection to linger; otherwise, the thoughts will grow roots and become more difficult to remove later. Whenever you feel rejected, reject the thought. Remember that the King of Kings has accepted you. He knows what it is to be rejected. He bore rejection so you wouldn't have to bear it.

Fear or Phobias – Another doorway is fear or phobias. Over nine hundred times the Bible tells us not to fear. Fear is not an attribute of heaven. It does not come from God our Father. Fear is opposite to faith. Fear negates faith. When Peter believed Jesus and stepped out of the boat, he walked on the water. As soon as he took his eyes off Jesus and looked at the wind, he opened the door to fear. Fear provided an avenue for negating faith and Peter began to sink.

A few years ago, strong winds blew some shingles off my roof. As I looked at the height of the roof, I said, *"There is no way I'm going up there to fix those shingles"* – *(Fear)*. Eventually, I spoke to my spirit, bought some glue and nails, put a ladder against the roof, got everything I needed to repair the roof and began quoting **2 Timothy 1:7–**

> *"For God has not given us a spirit of fear, but of power and of love and of a sound mind."*

I quoted that scripture all the way up the ladder, while I was fixing the shingles and all the way down. Challenge yourself then, to replace fear with faith by using God's word. If you have a fear or any phobia, start using faith to counteract it; even fear of mice or spiders.

Lust – Another doorway is lust. This does not only mean sexual lust. Many things in our culture appeal to the flesh. When we seek to satisfy our fleshly desires, that constitutes lust as well. Sometimes *Holy Spirit* tells us not to purchase an item. We may be able to afford the item, but if we just have to have the latest gadget or the latest fashion, our enemy will use that lustful desire against us. Lust could also relate to simple things like always wanting to have our way in a relationship or even in the Church.

Pursue becoming more mindful of the treasures in the celestial city and less attracted to the material things of this world. Jesus said:

> *"Store up for yourselves treasures in heaven, where moths and vermin do not destroy, and where thieves do not break in and steal. For where your treasure is, there your heart will be also."*

– **Matthew 6:20-21** *(NIV)*

Treasure in heaven is the most important accomplishment in life, so set your eyes on it. Someone may criticize you for being so heavenly minded until you're no earthly good. Does it really matter if they are right? The seasoned Christian who has spent years sending up material to furnish their mansion, will gradually desire to see and occupy their mansion more than any type of abode they have here on earth.

> *"For what shall it profit a man, if he shall gain the whole world, and lose his own soul?"*
> **– Matthew 8:36**

Money – This doorway hinges closely to lust.

> *"For the love of money is the root of all kinds of evil. And some people, craving money, have wandered from the true faith and pierced themselves with many sorrows."*
> **– 1 Timothy 6:10** *(NLT)*

Money is not the issue here. We need money to run ministry, but some pastors forfeit the *Gates of Pearls* for money. They use the Church even in unethical ways, just to increase the size of their bank account. Jesus was so upset with this mentality; He whipped the money changers and ran them out of the Temple.

> *"Is it not written, My house shall be called of all nations the house of prayer? But ye have made it a den of thieves."*
> **– Mark 11:17**

So, be careful how you use money. It is better to be poor and go to heaven than to be rich and miss the gates.

Sexual promiscuity – Often, children who were sexually abused grow to become sexual offenders as well. As a child, someone forced them and they were powerless to resist. Often, this sense of powerless or a desire to build a wall to resist it stays with them through their adult life. This wall also constitutes an open doorway. Closing this doorway is an uphill struggle for them, but they must close it and then keep it closed. There is much help available today in the professional and religious fields for people who are struggling in this area. I strongly suggest that people who have been sexually abused should utilize one or both of these avenues.

Through my book *"Thoughts For The Hurting Heart,"* God is challenging some people to stop covering their childhood abuse and to address the daunting psychological effect it has caused. Almost in tears, a lady in her sixties shared that her first child was conceived when she was sexually abused at age sixteen by her Aunt's husband. Although he had been dead a long time, the pain he inflicted was obviously much alive in her.

People who have not experienced sexual abuse may not readily empathize with these hurting individuals. Sometimes Christians are insensitive in this area as well. They may wonder why is it that this person can't just get over it. Or, why can't this person stop sinning? Or, why can't they stop going back into prostitution or homosexuality? For many of these individuals, quitting this behavior is usually very difficult. From a spiritual perspective, the problem is even more acute.

All types of sexual misconduct originate with Satan. Sexual abuse *(rape)* is the most unfortunate, but pornography, adultery, homosexuality, fornication, bestiality, wife swapping and all types of sexual orgies are satanically motivated. Often, under these circumstances, the sexual act of itself provides a direct access or a non

restricted doorway to demons. Sometimes, demons actually transfer from one individual to the other during this type of sexual intercourse. That's why it is difficult for such people to just get over it or to just stop committing those acts. They are driven by inner evil. Very often they want to stop, but the inner forces drive them, push them and sometimes even threaten them.

Even some Christians turn their face from these things, thinking that it's better not to know anything about this or worst; that they don't need to get involved with such matters. The reality is that many people are under bondages caused by sexually transferred demons and desperately need deliverance. Honest, dedicated, able and willing Christians need to be in place to help them – to pray with them and help them through to victory.

If you have been sexually abused and desire deliverance from inner forces, persevere and seek professional and spiritual help. If you fall again into Satan's trap, don't stay there. Get back up and start the fight all over again. Confess loudly that *"you are the righteousness of God in Christ Jesus"* – **2 Corinthians 5:21**. Don't ever give up! Ask *Holy Spirit* to help you as well and He will help you overcome. He will help you reach the *Gates of Pearls*.

Games – Some games provide a doorway as well. If you look at some of the characters in some video games, you don't need anyone to tell you where they originate. Sometimes research of their names reveals this as well. We should research games before we purchase them for our children. We don't want to inadvertently open any doorways for them. The Ouija board for example, gives answers. Now, a piece of wood or plastic cannot give answers. What or who is behind the characters of the board? It will benefit us greatly if we research these things.

Books and Movies – Some Christians may contradict this. The world's culture has so impacted us we agree wholeheartedly with its philosophy that books and movies are just literature or works of art. Believers must observe God's standard in all aspects of life; especially in the areas of education and entertainment.

Two years ago an acclaimed movie depicted the plight of African American women. Many Christians went to see this movie. Some said they were in tears as they watched, and they recommended it as a *"must see"* movie. When the DVD version became available, a Christian minister shared it with my wife. We started to watch it, but stopped relatively soon after it started. The language - the swearing and the vulgarity bothered our spirits. We wondered how Christians could watch such offensiveness. I remembered that Christians also subscribe to adult TV. They've gotten so used to vulgarity; it doesn't bother their spirit any longer. They have opened doorways to Satan and he is sitting comfortably in their hearts. They still think they are on their way to the holy city. If however, they don't kick the devil out and keep the door closed, they will not see the *Gates of Pearls*. To see those precious, holy gates don't be afraid to draw the line and separate from X rated material. If the world rated material as X, Christians should observe an even higher standard.

Magic – Magic is the playful tease to the broader, deeper arena of witchcraft. Have you ever wondered why Harry Potter books sold by the millions? The market attraction was that they grasped children's attention, fascinated them and got them to read. Magic will always seem harmless, but it is a small doorway that if opened can lead to witchcraft and other types of Satanism.

Shelly *(not her real name)* who reached one of the highest positions in witchcraft *(Regional Bride of Satan)*, started at a

church fair – learning how to read tea leaves and people's palms. By the time she came to Christ she had been involved in demonic sexual activity, astral projection and levitating. She had also destroyed over a hundred Christian churches.

Watch for doorways that magic opens, then close them and keep them closed. Indulgence in magic is detrimental to those desiring to see the *Gates of Pearls*. Father strongly forbids patronizing palm readers, psychics, fortune tellers and all areas of witchcraft. He commanded Israel not even to allow a witch to live – **Exodus 22:18**. Bible history shows that God detests involvement in these areas. We will have no excuse if we indulge in them.

Objects – Various objects serve as doorways as well. We must rid our homes of them as we become aware of them. The list of these includes some types of sculptures. You should research even the type of Christian jewelry you wear because some jewelry attracts demons. I know I'm going for the jugular now, but you should discard all religious images if you have any. Many of them are magnets for demons. I don't know which images attract demons and which do not, so get rid of them all. Argue if you want to, but my rebuttal would be: Do you want to see the *Gates of Pearls*? Also, please discard any object that is suppose to bring you good luck. Usually, these things have ungodly connotations.

Observances – Some doorways include certain observances. Halloween. It may be marketed as fun and it may be as American as apple pie, but everything about Halloween identifies it with the kingdom of darkness. Many Christians join in this celebration every fall. Please take the time to research it. God warned Israel not to meddle with satanic observances and celebrations. We would be wise to separate ourselves from them as well.

Kwanzaa – I had a lively, heated discussion about this at Bible school. One of my fellow students *(a school teacher)* argued strong and long in support of it. I challenged her to research it and get back to me. She was very apologetic the next week. I've always admired people who take the time to research a matter and are willing to accept the answers they find. One former atheist attorney, when faced with Jesus' claims to be Lord, pondered that in the courtroom everything was based on evidence. He then spent his own money investigating Jesus' claims. He is now a leading pro-lific Christian speaker. Christians especially should always seek for truth and put it above all beliefs.

Secret Societies – Some devout and tenured Christians are members of secret societies. If you are a Christian and have membership in a lodge, please consider which side of the fence you're on. For example, if you don't know the origin of the Masons it will do you much good to research it. Compare your initiation into the lodge with that of witchcraft as well.

Eastern Religions and Practices – Entertaining any non Christian religion can constitute a doorway. Jesus said:

> *"I am the way, the truth, and the life. No one comes to the Father except through Me."*

> – **John 14:6** *(NKJV)*

Jesus is the only way to heaven. Jesus stated emphatically that anyone else is a thief and a robber. Some religions promote healthy practices and some have gained acclaimed acceptance in our Western culture, but be cautious to engage in them. *Kung fu*, meditation *(blanking the mind)*, acupuncture, yoga, some diets, religious practices like libations to ancestors, repetitious prayers and chanting is not a comprehensive list, but research them while

soliciting *Holy Spirit's* guidance. He knows every subtle doorway; even the ones we are not aware of. He will help you identify them.

Social Doorways – This is a broad spectrum but some of them include:

Unforgiveness – This is probably the most challenging doorway to close, so it is the most devastating. Sadly, it will cost many Christians their crown. It will be the sole reason why they won't see the *Gates of Pearls*, yet forgiveness is easy. Just forgive! Jesus stated insistently in **Mark 11:26**:

> *"But if ye do not forgive, neither will your Father which is in heaven forgive your trespasses."*

Unforgiveness is like drinking poison with the hope that the person who did you wrong dies from it. It is allowing someone to live in your heart rent free. It doesn't matter if you are one hundred percent right and they are one hundred and fifty percent wrong. If you want to see the *Gates of Pearls* you must forgive them. Ask *Holy Spirit* to help you if you find it too hard to forgive them. Watch out! You are going to be amazed at how well He does His work.

Anger – In **Ephesians 4:26-27**, the Word of God says:

> *"Be ye angry, and sin not: let not the sun go down upon your wrath: Neither give place to the devil."*

Although the Bible allows for anger, limitations are set in place. Anger should not encroach on sin. By sundown, anger must have subsided – no exceptions! Notice that **verse 27** tells us plainly *not to give place to the devil*. Anger is a doorway that Satan will

use for his advantage even among Christian leaders. I credit *Holy Spirit* for teaching me this. I credit Him for showing me in advance when a situation that will irritate me is coming up, so I can head it off by prayer and rejecting it vocally.

Some pastors have a reputation of *"the one not to make angry."* Some stop two millimeters short of cursing when they are upset. Some even spit and grind their teeth, their blood pressure rises to almost stroke level and the adjutants have to coerce them into taking a seat to calm down. We understand the need for the Church to be run in a businesslike and orderly manner, but some leaders are sticklers for perfection and no one under them dare step out of line. Many leaders will miss the gates because of this; not because they strove for excellence, but because of uncontrolled anger. Moses fell short of entering the Promised Land because of his anger problems. He killed an Egyptian in anger. He smote the rock in anger. Please! Close all doors of anger.

Partiality – Showing partiality is a doorway that the Lord Jesus tells us not to open. We must be careful not to act like the world in this respect. In some churches today, some members get above average recognition and promotion because of their financial status. This action is very un-Christian, as it leads to an atmosphere of division and class separation. In **John 3:16,** God showed no partially when He sent Jesus, *"that whosoever believeth in Him should not perish but have everlasting life."* Embrace this non-partial demeanor, so you won't open this doorway.

James 2:3 *(NIV)* specifies:

> *"If you show special attention to the man wearing fine clothes and say, "Here's a good seat for you," but say to the poor man, "You stand there" or "Sit*

on the floor by my feet," have you not discriminated among yourselves and become judges with evil thoughts?"

This encourages us to shun partiality and to treat the poor with the same respect as the rich. Ask *Holy Spirit* to show you if you have this door open. If you do, please close it quickly.

Pride – Partiality and pride relate closely to each other. Pride keeps us away from intimacy with the *Lord Jesus Christ* and it may prevent some from crossing the finish line. We may be dedicated Christians, but pride hinders our spiritual development. **Proverbs 16:18** says:

"Pride goeth before destruction and an haughty spirit before a fall."

When pride resides in our hearts, God has to reveal it to us; otherwise, we wouldn't know it. Others can see it in us, but we can't see it in ourselves because it makes up our personality.

- *God has to show us* that we look down on others.
- *God has to show us* that we like to associate only with people whom society considers successful.
- *God has to show us* that the things we do (even in the Church) we do them only for recognition.
- *God has to show us* that our title is just a title and not a passport to heaven.

How many of us would mop our church's kitchen floor even though there is a paid custodian? **Psalms 138:6** says:

"Though the LORD is great, He cares for the humble, but He keeps His distance from the proud."

We can learn from the example Jesus left us. He was the most powerful man in the room, but He didn't sit and wait to be served. He put aside His kingly attire, wrapped a towel around His waist, washed and wiped His disciples' feet. Can you imagine the *Lord*, the *King of glory*, the creator stooping down to wash man's feet? That's a lesson in humility.

"Humble yourselves therefore under the mighty hand of God, that He may exalt you in due time."

– 1 Peter 5:6

Can Father depend on you to leave your league of friends, associates or business professionals at the mega Church, and serve at a local Church where the highest ranking member is an ordinary blue collar worker? A local Church is also a viable part of the body of Christ. It needs you. It needs your expertise; it needs your financial assistance and it needs your education and business skills. Will pride help the mega Church to upgrade to the most expensive sound system, but cause the local Church to close its doors because of a lack of patrons? Jesus loves the members of local churches just as much as members of any other Church. Humility counteracts pride. Ensure that humility is checked off on your list before you get to the gates.

Racism – We have pushed racism under the rug rather than address and eradicate it. We develop a bias from the culture that reared us. One of the most repulsive and visible signs of bias is racism between the black and white races. The world is guilty of this hideous crime. The plain, cold, hard facts are that although America outlawed segregation many decades ago, Sunday mornings still displays silent but active segregation.

- Think of the many white Christians who would not join a black Church.

- Think of the many black Christians who would not join a white Church.

Bias is a learned behavior, so we can discard it. Let us truly follow *Christ* and love and embrace people regardless of their color, race or ethnic background. Let's close the *doorway of racism*.

Religious Bias – We need to look candidly at this. I understand the need for commitment to what we believe. I understand also the specific and unbending requirements for entrance to heaven, but some denominations have taken this too far. They have become narrow minded in their thinking. Some will tell you that unless you share their religious beliefs and practices, there is no hope for you. Calvinists disagree with Armenians over whether a Christian can lose his or her salvation. Armenians disagree over baptism, the church's name, women in leadership roles, speaking in tongues, Trinitarian or Oneness baptism and many other matters that often serve only to divide us.

Let us be honest and practical. Let's use the plain common sense that God gave us. When did our denomination start? What is the status then, of all those Christians who died before the start of our church organization? Did they all go to hell because their baptism was different or their Church was called by a different name? Jesus knocked down all religious barriers so that anyone can make it to heaven. The basic requirement for heaven is to believe in the Lord Jesus Christ and establish a personal relationship with Him after repenting of our sins. Those of us who embrace these base principles should not allow our differences to divide us.

Jesus set up the Church, not a denomination. It is annoying that some Christians do not validate my salvation because I am a United Holy Church of America, Pentecostal Trinitarian. I am passionate about what I believe and I know that I am saved and that Jesus validates my salvation. I have concluded then that I should not think the same way as those who do not validate me, but to accept those who embrace the base principles of salvation. I have concluded also that if they are in error about the legitimacy of my salvation, there may be some things I believe that are not necessarily pertinent to salvation either. I am sure that those who cross the finish line will all be Christians and I am sure that no single Christian denomination has the monopoly on who will cross that line. Let's look away from the religious biases that divide us then, and unite to strengthen each other.

Lying – By words or actions. Lying is not an attribute of heaven. **Revelation 21:27** confirms this:

> *"And there shall in no wise enter into it anything that defileth, neither whatsoever worketh abomination, or maketh a lie."*

The systems of this world are increasingly pressuring us to lie. The person who looks you in the face and lies seems to be the one who succeeds in today's culture. Many institutions today seem to punish people for speaking the truth, but gate seekers must not succumb to cultural pressure. Even on the verge of the cross Jesus spoke the truth, so always speak the truth. It will make a big difference down the road.

Stealing – Among other things, taking things that are not our own from our workplace, from department stores or filing fraudulently on our taxes constitutes stealing. We also steal from

God when we do not pay tithes and offerings – **Malachi 3:8**. Some people argue against this but God's people should finance God's house. Over the years I have noticed that Christians who won't pay their tithes experience all kinds of financial problems. But those who strive to be obedient to God in this area, God opens the windows of heaven and pours blessings on them. I assure you that those who make it to the finish line are all tithers. Be a giver that God loves--a cheerful giver.

Complacency – We must ardently watch this subtle doorway. Over the years, I have seen people come to Christ with fervor and a desire to please Him. Soon after, they begin to rely on their own perception of Christian principles and biblical interpretations. *"I don't think.... or, I don't believe…."* are early signs of complacency. They are falling into a trap that only they themselves can climb out. Unfortunately, many do not. Note the words they use identify them with the deceiver. Note the similarities in their self promotion and self perception of divine principles. In **Isaiah 14:13-14** *(NLT)*, Lucifer *(the one who is deceiving them)* used these same self promoting assertions.

> *"**I will** ascend to heaven and set my throne above God's stars. **I will** preside on the mountain of the gods far away in the north. **I will** climb to the highest heavens and be like the Most High."*
>
> Emphasis is mine

Be alert not to trust your assessment of Godly principles. Pay special attention if you begin to think that you know the way to heaven and that it is not as stringent as those old Christians think it is. Reject thoughts of skipping church to do more important things on Sundays. Discard insinuations that you can slip away, sin and

get back without being noticed.   Shun complacency because it can be devastation.

> *"Not everyone who says to Me, 'Lord, Lord!' will enter the kingdom of heaven, but only the one who does the will of My Father in heaven."*
>
> **– Matthew 7:21** *(HCSB)*

The Bible has object lessons for us, to warn us against opening doorways that will invoke God's anger. As we trace the biblical history, we see that God intended for Israel to be the people who would adhere to Him and demonstrate principles of holiness. God made various concessions at times, but ultimately, He required absolute holiness and strict adherence to His laws. Some incidents seemed petty; the corresponding judgments seemed too harsh, but these were documented so we would know the seriousness of God's commands.

> *"All these things happened to them as examples— as object lessons to us—to warn us against doing the same things; they were written down so that we could read about them and learn from them in these last days as the world nears its end."*
>
> **– 1 Corinthians 10:11** *(TLB)*

While Joshua led Israel to one of its greatest victories, Achan took a Babylonian robe, 200 silver coins, and a bar of gold and hid them in his tent. This seemed petty, but people lost their lives because of it. One man sinned, but God told Joshua, *"Israel has sinned."* Achan's seemingly little sin cause the death of his entire family as well.

While Israel was bringing back the *Ark of God* that had been stolen, the cart stumbled. Uzzah reached out to prevent it from falling.

> *"And the anger of the LORD was kindled against Uzzah; and God smote him there for his error; and there he died by the ark of God."*
>
> **– 2 Samuel 6:7**

In **2 Samuel 24,** David counted the people and seventy thousand men lost their lives because of his actions. All these seemed petty, but they were serious enough to invoke God's anger and caused many to lose their lives. Doorways therefore, can be detrimental. As *Holy Spirit* speaks and shows us doorways, please close them. The sooner the better!

How To...

These are only some of the doorways to the soul. There may be many more than these listed, but we have *Holy Spirit* to show us all of them.

Search for truth. Search for it with an honest, open heart. Also, research some of the topics discussed in this chapter. Be prepared to close doorways to some cultural associations, celebrations, festivals and secular entertainment. Reaching the *Gates of Pearls* is more important than any of these things.

- Repeatedly remind yourself that your soul has doorways and that you are responsible for guarding them.
- Whenever you feel rejected, reject the thought.
  Remember that the *King of Kings* has accepted you.

- Sever all ties with discouragement.
- If you have been sexually abused, don't be apprehensive about seeking spiritual and professional help.
- If you fall into Satan's trap, don't remain there. Get back up and start the fight all over again. Repeatedly confess that you are the righteousness of God in Christ.
- Research books, games, movies, artwork and jewelry before you purchase them. Avoid X rated entertainment.
- Separate yourself from celebrations of any other God.
- Challenge yourself to replace fear with faith by using God's word. If you have a fear or a phobia, start exercising your faith to counteract it.
- Forgive others. Love people of all races, status and cultures.
- Never entertain partiality or pride.
- Shun *complacency* and daily **strive to please God**.

"Keep and guard your heart with all vigilance and above all that you guard, for out of it flows the springs of life."

– **Proverbs 4:23** *(AMP)*

MY PERSONAL THOUGHTS & INSPIRATIONS

_____

_____

_____

_____

CHAPTER 6
CLOSING DOORWAYS

It is not enough just to identify doorways to the soul. It is more important that we know how to guard them and how to keep them closed. I have interspersed some of the guidelines for closing them in the previous chapter. Now, we are going to look at some important ways to close them and keep the enemy out.

Psalms 119:105 says:

"Thy word is a lamp unto my feet, and a light unto my path."

A sure way to close doorways is by memorizing *God's word*. We can quote the word if we memorize it. In the wilderness, Jesus quoted the *Word of God* to counteract temptation. Satan quoted the Word also; only however, to receive a smashing rebuttal and rebuke as Jesus quoted the Word again. It was a match of words, but Jesus conquered because He is *God's son*. We are also God's sons, so the Word of God in our hearts, in our brains and in our mouths is a lethal weapon against our enemy.

In **Ephesians 6:17**, Paul said God's word is *the sword of the Spirit*. The *sword* is a vital part of our armor. With it, we defend ourselves and attack our enemies. I encourage young Christians to memorize the *Word of God*. Much of the scripture that is indelibly written in my brain, I memorized when I was young. If you're to be a successful runner, memorize God's word.

> *"This Book of the Law shall not depart from your mouth, but you shall meditate in it day and night, that you may observe to do according to all that is written in it.* **For then you will make your way prosperous, and then you will have good success***."*

> – **Joshua 1:8** emphasis is mine

If we memorize the Word it will be easy for us to quote. As illustrated by Jesus in the wilderness contest, quoting the Word is critical if we are to defeat our enemy. I have learned to quote the Word against sickness as well. Often I quote **Matthew 8:17** –

> *"That it might be fulfilled which was spoken by Esaias the prophet, saying, Himself took our infirmities, and bare our sicknesses."*

Satan has no choice but to back away when a believer verbalizes the Word of God. Remember the Word of God is our sword. It is our weapon of offence. Satan must exit and stay out when we use the sword *(Word of God)* against him. Vocalize the Word!

Reading God's Word

Read God's word! *Read God's word!* READ GOD'S WORD!

Along with prayer, strive to read God's word daily. Don't read the Bible only to hear God's voice; read chunks of it at a time to feed and enrich your spirit man. Sometimes when you are struggling to close a door, our adversary will make your schedule busy so you wouldn't have time to read the Word. Get an audio Bible and listen

to it on your way to work. Get away from the office during your lunch break and read the Word. Stress level in the corporate environment is high and especially if you are in management you don't have enough hours in a day, but prioritize lunch (reading the Word) breaks. Get away! Get out of the office! Even Jesus got away from the crowds sometimes.

> *"Then Jesus suggested, "Let's get away from the crowds for a while and rest." For so many people were coming and going that they scarcely had time to eat."*
>
> **– Mark 6:31** *(TLB)*

Obeying God's Word

There is no way around this. There is no substitute for obedience to God's word. Sacrifice, tears, regrets or pleading will not suffice either. Saul's tragic end depicts this:

> *"And Samuel said, hath the LORD as great delight in burnt offerings and sacrifices, as in obeying the voice of the LORD? Behold, to obey is better than sacrifice, and to hearken than the fat of rams."*
>
> **– 1 Samuel 15:22**

God's kingdom is built on obedience while Satan's is built on rebellion. God's children must be obedient. Disobedience forms a great doorway to the soul. Disobedience derails us and leaves us like a train wreck. We can even lose our life when we disobey God's word. **Proverbs 29:1** says:

"He, that being often reproved hardeneth his neck, shall suddenly be destroyed, and that without remedy."

God rejected Saul because of disobedience, but blessed Abraham, David and other patriarchs because of their obedience.

- When God said, *"Come out from among them and be separate"*, we must obey that command.
- When God said, *"You shall have no other Gods but me"*, we must obey that too.
- When God says: *"be ye holy for I am holy"*, we must be holy.

Gate seekers therefore, must be different from fellow city dwellers. We must love one another, forgive one another and be obedient to our church leaders. **Hebrews 13:17** says:

"Obey them that have the rule over you, and submit yourselves: for they watch for your souls, as they that must give account, that they may do it with joy, and not with grief: for that is unprofitable for you."

We may reject our pastor's discipline, run to another Church and bask in the less stringent conditions there, but we cannot entertain a disobedient attitude if we want to see the *Gates of Pearls*. Some of us may have to go back to our former Church and apologize.

It is natural; it is part of our human nature *(especially adults)* to resent and resist anything or anyone we think is trying to control us. We must bring this area of our human nature under subjection to God's will. The Church is not set up to control or exercise authority over anyone. The Church is designed to fashion us and prepare us for heaven.

"And he gave some, apostles; and some, prophets; and some, evangelists; and some, pastors and teachers; **For the perfecting of the saints, for the work of the ministry, for the edifying of the body of Christ:** *Till we all come in the unity of the faith, and of the knowledge of the Son of God, unto a perfect man, unto the measure of the stature of the fullness of Christ."*

– **Ephesians 4:11-13** emphasis is mine

We must obey those who are placed in authority over us in the Church. This is God's word and our choice is to obey if we want to remain on the path to glory. God's word:

"Is a lamp unto our feet, and a light unto our path."
– **Psalms 119:105**

We need the Word to light the pathway to glory; nothing else will! When we obey God's word He will stamp our passport at the gates.

Beware of Backsliders

In **1 Kings 13**, Israel was in an impoverished, backslidden condition. God sent a young prophet with a message to the king and to prophesy about the coming of *King Josiah*, who would restore Israel. In **verse 13**, God told the young prophet, *"Eat no bread, nor drink water, nor turn again by the same way that thou camest."* Even when the king offered him lunch, he refused and obeyed God's instructions instead. But he met a backslidden prophet who touted that he also heard from God. If this was true, why didn't God use him to take the message to the King instead? This should have been a telltale sign for the young prophet. I believe, out of humility and respect for his elder, he allowed the old prophet to coerce him into staying and eating. As soon as he started back on his journey a lion attacked him and killed him. Deception cost the young prophet his life while the backslidden prophet *(the one he looked up to)* was still alive.

Watch for these types of backsliders – broken down vehicles. They cause traffic jams, accidents and even fatalities on this highway to glory. They can cause your death as well. If you are not careful and prayerful, you won't recognize them because they are sandwiched between other believers. Remember in the kingdom parables Jesus spoke about the wheat and the tares growing together?

> *"Allow both to grow together until the harvest; and in the time of the harvest I will say to the reapers, First gather up the tares and bind them in bundles to burn them up; but gather the wheat into my barn."*

> **– Matthew 13:30** *(NASB)*

Do not go around trying to categorize who are wheat and who are tares; just look at the kind of fruit people are producing. You'll recognize them by their fruits. An apple tree cannot produce oranges; neither can a mango tree produce bananas. Be cautious in taking advice from the tares. As in the case with the backslidden prophet, they can cause your premature death; yet they continue living and will have a chance to get back on the road. They may make it to the gates of the city while you may not. How do you feel when you are driving behind a car that is going at 5 miles per hour and

the stop light up ahead is about to change; the driver speeds up just before the light changes and get through the light, but you get stuck? It's the same with these tares *(backsliders)*. Don't allow them to deceive you. They may have a chance to repent; you may not.

Brother Mike, *(not his real name)* received salvation after many years of drug addiction and incarceration. He began to grow spiritually until one of these tares got to him. Of course, they shared with him their side of all the wrongdoings of the church leadership. He was not strong enough to separate the good from the bad. Gradually, he began to find excuses for not attending church services. Within less than two years, he was back in prison. He allowed a backslider to turn his mind away from the truth and the Church; hopefully, not from God.

Please be cautious also about entertaining gossip. Be wise to always look for the fruits of the Spirit – **Galatians 5:22-23**. Treat backsliders in a Christ-like manner. Try to win them back to Christ, but close all doorways that they can possibly use to deceive you. You may lose a few friends when you take a stand for righteousness, but you'll protect your soul.

Repentance

Repentance is necessary when we realize that we have committed sin. Repentance is a failsafe way to close doorways. Repentance is essential for regeneration, but there is a need for ongoing repentance as well. This does not mean that Christ's blood is not efficacious. We sin through our words, our thoughts and our deeds. **Isaiah 6** shows also that the closer we get to God His light reveals more of our sinful nature. As we become aware of sins we commit after we are saved, we should repent of them. The road to the gates requires repentance for sins and making a clean break from them.

> *"Let not sin therefore rule as king in your mortal (short-lived, perishable) bodies, to make you yield to its cravings and be subject to its lusts and evil passions."*

> **– Romans 6:12** *(AMP)*

Some Christians attend church regularly, sing on the choir, and serve on various church committees, yet they see nothing wrong with a little lie here and there. Fornication, adultery and even homo-sexuality are perfectly okay with some Christians. Some curse, swear, gamble or drink heavily and yet believe they will make it to heaven. Satan is deceiving many into thinking that they can keep sinning and still pass through the gates of the holy city. Repentance however, opens our eyes, closes all the door-ways to the soul and helps us to make it to the city of God.

Rest Stop

Before I close this chapter, I must highlight a sneaky door-way that we all need to be aware of. Busyness! This is not only secular busyness, but busyness in ministry as well. We can be so busy working for God that we don't have time for God. Rest stops however, are on the highway; not lazy, do nothing stops, but rest stops. Occasionally, we must take time to rest and rejuvenate.

Spiritual Rest

The Almighty creator worked six days and rested on the seventh day. To those of us who are involved in ministry, let me remind you that Jesus already died for the world. If the world is not saved by Jesus' death, we are not going to save it either. It makes no sense working so hard in the Church that we don't have enough time for God. In **Luke 10:41-42**, Jesus told Martha:

"You are worried and troubled about many things. But one thing is needed, and Mary has chosen that good part, which will not be taken away from her."

Don't prioritize saving the world and over-extend yourself.

Pastors, take a spiritual rest. You can't fix everything. Leave some things undone just to spend time with God. A spiritual rest is not laziness; it is just being sensible. When you die, the congregation will find another pastor. Your reward is in heaven not here on earth. Focus on your reward, not on laboring for the reward.

"He thought it was better to suffer for the sake of Christ than to own the treasures of Egypt, for he was looking ahead to his great reward."

– Hebrews 11:26 *(NLT)*

Some pastors are realizing tremendous success in their ministry, yet they've grown spiritually poor. They may have a mega Church and a worldwide TV ministry, but they are so busy they don't have time for personal devotion. God is a jealous God. He wants us to spend time with Him. Strive to spend at least one hour each day with Him. Take a spiritual rest!

Secular Rest

You are on your way to glory, but don't be so heavenly minded that you're no earthly good. You still live on Planet Earth – Planet Earth that Jesus created; so enjoy it. Heaven or hell was not made for us; earth was. Yes, we are on our way to heaven, but Jesus had to renovate heaven to accommodate us after Adam forfeited his inheritance. In **John 14:2-3** Jesus said:

> *"I go to prepare a place for you. And if I go and prepare a place for you, I will come again and receive you to Myself; that where I am, there you may be also."*

...but originally, earth was created for us.

How astounding to see the white snow peaks of mountains or the majesty of great waterfalls—thundering down, forming rivers and lakes of various shapes and sizes—trees of all shapes and sizes blossoming in a magnificent array of all colors of the rainbow, filling the air with varieties of unmatched fragrances. There is no other planet known like Planet Earth.

Planet Earth was created specifically for us, with a place here for everyone's fancy. All over the world are numerous natural

vacation spots – places of relaxation and fun. God must have had us in mind when He created them, so take time to enjoy them. Take a vacation. Spend time with your family and friends. Don't step over the line and commit sin, but loosen up! Even when all hell breaks loose, relax sometimes. The devil will always be the devil. He is not going to get saved! He will continue to do devil things until he is thrown into the bottomless pit, so stop worrying about some things. Worry can't change anything other than give you ulcers. Take time to rest. Remember that the battle is not yours; it is the Lord's. Don't be busy trying to close one door and leave another wide open.

How To...

Closing a doorway may not always be easy, but as long as you close it, it is easier to keep it closed. Fight to close any doorways you have realized while reading these chapters. Fight with everything you have available to you. Remember the *Word of God* is our sword. It is our weapon of offence and defense. Satan must exit and stay out when we use the *Word of God*. **Read** God's word. **Memorize** God's word. **Quote** the Word when sickness, depression or anything contrary to God's word comes.

Feed and enrich your spirit by setting aside a time for daily prayer and Bible reading. If you have a busy schedule, get away from the office during your lunch break and read the Word.

Saturate your spirit with the *Word of God*. The enemy will find it difficult to stick around under such conditions.

Along with using the Word, fight with prayer, fasting, praising and worshiping God and meditating. You may also want to seek environments where the gifts of the Spirit are operating. All the gifts of the Godhead are for our benefit, especially under these circumstances. There is much deception around, so exercise caution and ensure *Holy Spirit's* guidance.

Based on the severity of the doorway you are trying to close, seek professional help as well. Do everything you can to guard your heart.

- Submit to your church leadership, but do not follow leaders who practice or condone sin.

- Keep a keen eye for backslidden Christians. Do not allow them to pull you away from God's principles.

- If you fall into sin *Holy Spirit* will convict you. Repent quickly.

- Take time to rest. Enjoy time with your family and friends. Enjoy some of the amenities this world has to offer.

- Close all doorways to your soul and keep them closed.

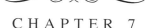

CHAPTER 7
WHO SPEAKS INTO YOUR LIFE

People with whom we cross paths and interact with in our lifetime, influence our demeanor, manipulate our relational aptitude, shape the way we react to others and affect our destiny. Some people can have positive influences on us. Positive influences help us to achieve greater heights than we normally would. Others can so negatively influence us that our personality reshapes and aligns itself to corroborate their negative behavior, resulting in failure in many areas of our lives.

When one turns to Christ and their lifestyle is changed for the better, it happens because someone influenced them. Someone spoke Christ's love into them and as they embraced the message they heard, they were changed by God's power. Many lives are different today because some preacher, teacher, or evangelist spoke into them. **So, who speaks into your life?**

- Esther allowed Mordecai to speak into her life. She became the queen of the great Persian Empire and saved her people from extinction..
- Elisha allowed Elijah to speak into his life and he received a double portion of Elijah's anointing.

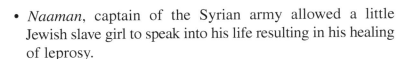

- *Naaman*, captain of the Syrian army allowed a little Jewish slave girl to speak into his life resulting in his healing of leprosy.
- The widow of Zarephath allowed Elijah to speak into her life and there was food on her table all through a famine.
- Mary allowed an angel to speak into her life and she gave birth to Jesus, the son God.

"And Mary said, Behold the handmaid of the Lord; be it unto me according to thy word."

– Luke 1:38

Two Types

During my years of pastoring, I've noted that I could distinguish between two distinct types within the congregation. In one group were those who allowed me *(my personality – my vision – my teachings)* to speak into their lives. Their spirits were open to me. They were like sponges – they absorbed whatever I taught.

As I overviewed the congregation and gauged individual spiritual fitness, I noted also that the ones in this group were maturing spiritually. As I watched them maturing and being blessed, I associated their growth with the fact that they allowed the man of God to influence them – to speak into their lives. They received the word; obeyed instructions; and submitted to leadership. God manifested His grace, His love, and His power in their lives and they experienced significant miracles also.

In the second group, were those whose minds were closed- –closed to instructions – closed even to teachings on faith – closed to the influence of my personality, my vision, and my teachings. Instead of embracing the *Word of God*, they rationalized instructions, and chose which items they would receive and which they would discard. As I also compared their spiritual aptitude, I noted that they remained spiritually shallow and many of them eventually walked away or backslid. Even the revealed, inspired and anointed Word of God did not influence them because their minds were closed to God's messenger. They did not allow the man of God to speak into their lives.

Evil and good coexist in the world. Since external forces and people influence our decision-making, we inadvertently allow either good or evil to influence us. We embrace one of these influences and reject the other. The first group embraced the good; therefore, growth and productivity resulted. The second group rejected the good and inadvertently embraced evil; therefore, stagnation and even backsliding resulted.

Sadly, in response to external influences, we all have an inherent tendency to cuddle negative behavior. So, even after we are *"born again,"* we must strive daily to pull away from our own natural tendencies to be critical of instructions, challenge authority, and being relatively self-confident in making decisions. That's why the Bible challenges us to renew our minds after we are saved: – **Romans 12:2**.

> *"And do not be conformed to this world, but be transformed by the renewing of your mind, that you may prove what is that good and acceptable and perfect will of God."*

If God commands us to renew our minds, the responsibility of getting rid of our old mindset and acquiring a new one rests on our own shoulders. We may be sincere in piety and religious devotion, yet we must daily renew our own minds. **Proverbs 3:5** *(NLT)* tells us:

> *"Trust in the LORD with all your heart; do not depend on your own understanding."*

This is not to say that we can't trust our own intellect; it implies that our intellect should corroborate the divine will of God and be always submissive to His Word.

Allow Your Pastor to Speak Into Your Life

In **Jeremiah 3:15** God said:

> *"And I will give you pastors according to mine heart, which shall feed you with knowledge and understanding."*

This means that God sends instructions to the body of Christ through pastors. I'm not implying that God speaks exclusively through pastors; it would be unbiblical and foolish even to think so.

God ordained Pastors

This verse explains that God uses the office of the pastor as a conduit to transfer knowledge and understanding to the body of Christ. From this, we may also conclude that since God ordained pastors to feed the congregation with knowledge and understanding, the congregation's responsibility is to receive the knowledge and understanding that God disseminates through their pastor. We may also deduce that:

- We develop spiritually as we receive knowledge and understanding through our pastor.
- We must embrace and apply the revealed Word of God to avoid spiritual stagnation.
- We must allow our pastor to speak into our lives.

To grow spiritually we must be connected to heaven. Our pastor is our link to spiritual growth and maturity. Our pastor may not be the most eloquent speaker, but he or she is our link to divine instructions. If you are not receiving knowledge and understanding through your pastor, check your own spirit to see if it is open to receive. If your spirit is open and receptive, then pray for your pastor that God would use him or her to establish the link and be the conduit for your spiritual nutrition. If your spirit is not open please adjust it now so that blessings can flow to you.

Peter's Personality

Peter had the reputation of being a hardhearted, stiff-necked, self-centered, self-made disciple – one who was set in his ways. Ironically, this type of personality possesses a unique ability to speak into others and inadvertently influence them into following. In **John 21:3**, because Jesus had been crucified and the future of His three and a half year movement seemed hopeless, *"Simon Peter saith unto them, I go a fishing. They say unto him, we also go with thee."* Although they all had been with Jesus for three and a half years, experiencing miracles beyond their wildest imagination, it is obvious here that Peter's negative personality spoke into their lives with a greater impact than all the words Jesus spoke to them during their years of training. When Peter was ready to give up on the movement, they all followed Peter because his personality obviously spoke louder than all the words spoken by the master Himself. Could this happen to you?

- Whose personality is speaking into your life?
- Are people with a Christ-like mindset influencing you?
- Does the spirit of Christ temper their personality?
- Who are your role models?

Allow the RIGHT person to speak into your life

So, who speaks into your life today – Christian friends, uncommitted Christians, Preachers, Evangelists? The fact that Peter was ready to go back to his old job so quickly, demonstrated that as of yet, he had not allowed the Lord Jesus to speak into his life, yet others allowed him to speak into their life. This shows that many lives will be changed when we allow the right person to speak into our life since our actions influence others as well.

The Patience of Jesus

Although Peter failed miserably, the Savior's welcoming arms were always open wide to him. Jesus illustrated this when He reinstated Peter after Peter had abandoned Him, denied that he knew Him, and lied repeatedly. In **John 21:15** *(NLT)*, we see Jesus ardently trying to speak into Peter, but receiving only a casual, lackadaisical response from him.

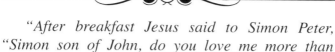

"After breakfast Jesus said to Simon Peter, "Simon son of John, do you love me more than these?" "Yes, Lord," Peter replied, "you know I love you." "Then feed my lambs," Jesus told him."

If we were in Jesus' shoes where He poured into Peter's life for over three years, yet received the type of response from him, we would probably turn away in frustration or in anger. But **John 21:16** *(TLB)* says:

"He repeated the question: "Simon, son of John, do you really love me?" "Yes, Lord!" Peter said, "You know I am your friend." "Then take care of my sheep."

Jesus was trying to speak into Peter's life, but Peter wasn't even listening! Jesus waited for an appropriate time to try again.

"After breakfast, Jesus said to Simon Peter, "Simon, son of John, do you love me more than these others?"

– **John 21:15** *(TLB)*

In my own words:

"Peter! You say you love me. When multitudes walked away and I asked the twelve if they would also go away, your response was: "To whom shall we go? You alone have the words that give eternal life, and we believe them and know you are the holy Son of God."

– **John 6:68-69** *(TLB)*

Peter, you also said as recorded in **Matthew 26:35** –

> *"Even if I must die with thee, (yet) will I not deny thee." But Simon, son of John, are you even my friend?"*

> *"Peter was grieved at the way Jesus asked the question this third time. He responded "Lord, you know my heart; you know I am," he said. Jesus said, "Then feed my little sheep."*

Peter, the self-centered, egotistic, proud, personality that influenced others to turn away from following Christ, was finally broken. Finally, Peter *(the rock)* allowed Jesus to speak into his life. After Peter allowed his personality to be tempered by the master, he was never the same. From that moment, Peter began to grow spiritually. He rose to a position of prominence and became the leader of the first Church. After he allowed Jesus to speak into his life, Peter found his purpose in life. Is the Lord Jesus speaking to you right now? Are you allowing Him to speak into your life?

> *"Incline your ear, and come unto me: hear, and your soul shall live; and I will make an everlasting covenant with you, even the sure mercies of David."*

– Isaiah 55:3

Allow the Savior to speak into your life. Your right response to Christ's speaking into your life will not only affect your whole demeanor and purpose in life; your changed personality will also positively influence others. Just as Jesus will use you to influence other lives, He will use others to influence you and speak into your life as well. On this side of heaven, you may not personally

(physically) meet Jesus as Peter did, but Jesus meets, interacts, and speaks to us through others just as well; sometimes in ways we least expect.

> *"I Jesus have sent mine angel to testify unto you these things in the churches. I am the root and the offspring of David, and the bright and morning star."*
>
> **– Revelation 22:16**

Jesus speaks to us in so many ways, but sometimes we can't hear Him because of the noise around us - Self pity noise, or noise of running after personal goals. But get away to a quiet place sometimes just to hear Him. This is not necessarily a physical quiet place. Sometimes we need to get to a spiritually quiet place – A place where we drop all personal, religious, traditional and inherited ideologies and just listen to Him.

Christian Material

Jesus speaks to us in various ways, but we must make personal investments to enhance our spiritual alertness. Along with the usual Christian observances, we should invest in other Christian material including books, testimonials, music, videos and various Christian media. This is critical in making us a more wholesome Christian. Everything that has a Christian label is not necessarily sanctioned by *Holy Spirit*, but there is much Holy Spirit inspired information today that can enhance our spiritual growth and stability. The internet for example, is a source of invaluable information that we can use to build our faith.

God will use others to bless us as we allow them to speak into our lives. Christians from all over the world are receiving visions, signs or out-of-body experiences. There is a lot of deception today, but do not close your mind to everyone who experiences these revelations. Trust *Holy Spirit* to lead you in all truth. A closed mind can be a closed door to information *Holy Spirit* is disseminating to make us more knowledgeable and better equipped to defend ourselves against the wiles of the devil.

In my book *"Thoughts From His Heart,"* I shared a story of a young lady who inherited a *familiar spirit.* She didn't know why she could see into the spirit realm, neither did she want the ability to do so. When she met me and shared her story, she was relieved that I understood her predicament. I was able to help her because I had already spent time on research in those areas. As we educate ourselves in the spiritual arena we'll not only strengthen our faith, we'll help others along the way. To help others on this journey gives us priceless joy. We must make the required investments.

I talked with a man who had been a Christian for many years, yet he was still struggling with Christianity's principles. His Muslim friends had influenced him so much that he was contemplating that Christianity was not the only way to heaven. As I conversed with him and searched for the reasons for his lack of soundness in the Christian faith, I discovered that he had not invested much in his personal Christian development. His pastor is a spirit filled anointed preacher who has also written inspiring Christian books, yet this man had not read any of them. I'm sure his pastor also disseminated vast amount of information and recommendations for Christian growth, but this man had not invested in those things that would have strengthen his faith. Since he didn't invest in the information that God made available for his development, he was an easy target for deceptive forces.

Don't follow this man's footsteps. Invest in various types of inspired Christian material so you will enhance your spiritual well-being. Allow Godly people, Godly environments and Godly things to speak into your life.

How To...

If you want to soar like eagles, then rise to where the eagles fly! Associate with those who can help you hear God's voice and let their tenacity influence you. Embrace people who speak spiritually positive things into your life! Find committed, word believing, Christians and hang out with them. Open yourselves to them so they can speak into your life and influence you. Then the spiritual blessings they enjoy will rub off on you as well. Trust *Holy Spirit* to lead you to the various media He is making available today and invest in it.

Find someone who can help you get a prayer through! Allow them to speak into your life. The benefits will be greater – much greater than you will ever imagine.

God bless you!

MY PERSONAL THOUGHTS &
INSPIRATIONS

CHAPTER 8
EFFORT, NOT PERFECTION

God sees all that we are going through. God knows when we've expended all our energy. He knows how long we've been striving with various issues. If He takes the time to count and record the number of hairs on our head, surely He is aware of every trial we face. God is perfect, but He does not expect us to be perfect. He only expects us to put forth our best effort. He expects us to–

> *"Make every effort to enter through the narrow door…"*
>
> – **Luke 13:24** *(NIV)*

When we come before God with an honest, humble, sincere heart and ask for His help, He helps us.

Salvation is free but it is not cheap.

Salvation cost Jesus His life. The ticket to redeem Adam's fallen generation cost heaven a great sacrifice. Jesus paid the cost for us to enter through the *Gates of Pearls*, but that does not mean that anyone can just relax and leisurely walk into heaven. Yes, our tickets were already paid for, but we encounter significant challenges while journeying to the gates.

> *"Be careful – watch out for attacks from Satan, your great enemy. He prowls around like a hungry, roaring lion, looking for some victim to tear apart. Stand firm when he attacks. Trust the Lord; and remember that other Christians all around the world are going through these sufferings too."*
>
> – **1 Peter 5:8-9** *(TLB)*

In **Matthew 19:24** Jesus said:

> *"It is easier for a camel to go through the eye of a needle, than for a rich man to enter into heaven."*

If you have the time and the energy to entertain arguments on the logistic of this statement you may do so, but whatever Jesus meant, the disciples interpreted it as impossible for anyone to make it to heaven. To them, the bar seemed too high; the prerequisites appeared unattainable and the road impossible! Jesus however, responded that with man it may seem impossible, but with God, all things are possible. So, someone is going to make it to heaven.

> *"Go in by the narrow gate.* ***For the wide gate has a broad road which leads to disaster and there are many people going that way****. The narrow gate and the hard road lead out into life and **only a few are finding it**."*
>
> – **Matthew 7:13-14** *(JB Phillips)* emphasis is mine

Although few will find the way to heaven's gates, no one ever said that you can't be among those who find it. I reiterate that the way to heaven is not as easy as portrayed in much of our Western Christian media, but making it there is possible.

However we look at the statement Jesus made regarding finding the way to heaven, it is obvious that those who find it will have to do some personal, private striving. This could generate controversy and arguments among Christian denominations, because it challenges doctrines that some people have been taught for generations. Well, I haven't lost my mind and I am certainly not anti-Evangelical or anti-Calvinist. I know that salvation is a gift from God and that we are saved by faith. But if you think you don't have to strive daily to maintain your spiritual position, please open your eyes. Although you are *"saved, sanctified and filled with the precious Holy Ghost,"* forces in the atmosphere are constantly placing obstacles in your way to prevent you from getting to heaven. If they knew they could not detour saved, sanctified, *Holy Ghost* filled believers, why would they even try?

In **2 Timothy 3:12**, Paul said:

> *"All that will live godly in Christ Jesus shall suffer persecution."*

Be prepared then, to strive, because striving is part of Christianity's package. No one is immune to the obstructions these forces place in our path, but we'll overcome them if we strive.

> *"For this I toil, striving with all the energy, which he mightily inspires within me."*
>
> – **Colossians. 1:29** *(RSV)*

Angels To Help

God knows that on our own we cannot make it, that's why He is looking for us to make an effort. Much help is available to us, but we have to make up our minds and settle in our spirits to daily put forth an effort in order to maintain our spiritual stability.

Jesus died for all our sins so we can be worthy to pass through the gates and Holy Spirit came as our helper. Angels have a unique role as well. God sent them to minister to us – to help us overcome all the artillery our enemy throws our way.

> *"For the angel of the Lord is a guard; he surrounds and defends all who fear Him."*
>
> **– Psalm 34:7** *(NLT)*

Angels are always with us, but they cannot do everything for us. There are rules of engagement within the spirit realm. Some things we must do for ourselves. We must submit to God and then resist the devil *(James 4:7)*. Angels do not violate our wills. In answer to someone's prayer, they work in authentic ways, but our wills and the effort we put forth prioritizes and determines what they can do for us. Angels perform astronomical tasks to protect us. Sometimes they use a little humor, like a little nail in the tire to delay us from a deadly accident down the road, but they always respect our wills.

Angels are one hundred percent committed to God. They work untiringly to perform His will. If in answer to your prayer, your cousin is assigned to them to aid her in accepting Christ, they will do everything in their power to guide her into places where she will hear the gospel. If she does not accept Christ when exposed to the gospel, they will start the process all over again. Giving up is not in their vocabulary. Performing God's will is their priority.

The Bible encourages us to treat strangers kindly because we may entertain angels unaware. Angels appeared on numerous occasions in the Bible. Maybe, you have unknowingly entertained one at some time. Don't expect to see angels as tall, glistening beings with a halo around their head and wings attached to their backs. Most likely, they will appear as ordinary humans and speak your language, even your dialect if you speak one. Angels come to church and document every detail – the time you arrive, the time you leave, how much money you gave, your attitude when you gave, how much attention you paid to the sermon and the comments you internalize in response to it.

Angels are ranked and assigned different functions. Michael is the archangel or chief angel and the captain of warring angels. Warring angels are those who fight against demon spirits and scatter them on our behalf. Without these army angels thwarting much of Satan's efforts, many of us would be disabled or even dead a long time ago. Some of us might not have been born had it not been for the work of these warring angels. Every Christian has at least one angel assigned to them. We should not pray to them, but it's okay to ask them to perform tasks for us sometimes.

> *"Are not the angels all ministering spirits (servants) sent out in the service [of God for the assistance] of those who are to inherit salvation?"*

> **– Hebrews 1:14** *(AMP)*

Gabriel is the captain of the messenger angels.

These travel at lightning speed with messages between heaven and earth. They specialize in carrying answers to prayers,

> *"And the angel answering said unto him, I am Gabriel, that stand in the presence of God; and am*

sent to speak unto thee and to shew thee these glad tidings."

– Luke 1:19

If our journey to the *Gates of Pearls* is to be successful we are going need much help from angels, but we must put forth an effort of our own. God knows we need help that's why He is not looking for perfection, only effort. If God was expecting perfection from us He would not have sent angels to help us.

Four Gospels

The four gospels demonstrate that God is not looking for perfection – just effort. Have you ever wondered why there are four Gospels about Jesus? If it was man's decision to write about Jesus, we would look for the most accurate information about Him and publish one document. Our perfection is however, often useless to God. Even Jesus didn't write a book about Himself. God allowed four different writers to write about Jesus. Each writer wrote to a different audience and God allowed their varying personalities to influence their version of the gospel. Some things therefore, are unique to each gospel, yet they all talk about Jesus. God accepted and blessed each writer's efforts so much that He included all four gospels in *His book* – **the Bible**.

Different Shapes and Sizes

Why an effort? Jesus knows that we all encounter many obstacles. He knows the obstacles we face may be as diverse as we are, but that they are all very real. They show up at different times

in our journey and always at inappropriate times. They come in various shapes and sizes, but they are not prejudiced. You have them, I have them, and the person you least suspect has them. Especially today, it seems like it doesn't take much for a Christian to give up, but God expects us to put forth an effort and stay in the race.

- ***Don't*** let obstacles define who you are.
- ***Don't*** let obstacles push you off the road.
- Obstacles may have ruined your past, but ***don't*** let them dictate your future.
- ***Don't*** let them drive you to the point of spiritual suicide.

….Run in such a way as to get the prize.

"Everyone who competes in the games goes into strict training. They do it to get a crown that will not last; but we do it to get a crown that will last forever. Therefore, I do not run like a man running aimlessly; I do not fight like a man beating the air."

– **1 Corinthians 9:24-26** *(NIV)*

Whatever obstacle you face, no matter how big it is, no matter how long it has hindered your progress, and no matter who is causing it, keep striving. ***Don't give up! Don't ever give up!*** Don't look for exit signs or excuses to justify quitting either. The gates are your destination and there is no other acceptable option.

"I press toward the mark for the prize of the high calling of God in Christ Jesus."

– **Philippians 3:14**

Complex But Conquerable

Life as a Christian is not always easy. If it was easy, almost everyone would be on their way to heaven. Remember Jesus said although many would try to get to heaven, only few would be successful. Those who will make it must put forth an effort. The very essence of the word effort implies that there is adversity, difficulty, danger, hardship and complexity. On this road, you cannot reach the next mountain top unless you pass through the valley: The dark valley--full of danger, difficulty, hardship and complexity, but you must always put forth an effort to make it through the valley, and then climb the steep hill to the next mountain top.

Satan challenges our efforts and tries to thwart our advancement. He believes that if he keeps the pressure on, eventually we are going to get frustrated and give up. Thank God, that Jesus is always a step ahead of him. Jesus paid for every accusation hurled against us, then dismantled all principalities and powers. Bless God! Bless God! Jesus brought us out of a horrible pit, placed us on the highway to glory and told us:

> *"Just keep walking. Don't focus on the trials and difficulties--Just keep walking. No weapon formed against you shall prosper. I have already overcome the world and I have paved the way to the Gates of Pearls, so just – keep – walking."*

> *"When you go through deep waters, I will be with you. When you go through rivers of difficulty, you will not drown. When you walk through the fire of oppression, you will not be burned up; the flames will not consume you."*

> **– Isaiah 43:2** *(NLT)*

Oh, that makes me want to shout! I wish you could finish this chapter, challenged and inspired to stay in the race all the way to the end. I wish you could be so energized that you could leap over walls! I hope you are convinced that even when all hell breaks loose and it looks like there is no way out, God is only looking for effort, not perfection.

How To ...

- *Make an effort!*—Read your Bible more than you have before.

- *Make an effort!*—Pray more than you have prayed in the past.

- *Make an effort!*—Be more honest with yourself and with God.

- *Make an effort!*—Overcome all temptations and trials.

- *Make an effort!*—Retreat from things that displeases God.

- *Make an effort!*—Be filled with the Spirit.

- *Make an effort!*—Experience God in all His fullness.

- *Make an effort!*—Quit trying to be perfect!

MY PERSONAL THOUGHTS & INSPIRATIONS

CHAPTER 9
WOUNDED IN THE HOUSE OF MY FRIENDS

In earlier chapters, we discussed conflict in the Church and doorways to the soul. We saw how devastating conflict can be and how doorways, if left open, can allow our enemy to detour us. The subject we're about to deal with touches both these areas, but it highlights how Christians can be personally affected by them. There is hardly a Christian who has not been affected by *"Wounds caused by other Christians."* I will expose how destructive this behavior is to Christians and show how to survive its tentacles.

Christians have a distasteful history of **shooting our wounded**.

Backstabbing and gossip is too alive and active among Christians today. Many people have turned away from the faith because of these social issues. This is disturbing because some of these people ran to the Church as a refuge from the soul discomfort of the world. Even if they were not raised in the Church, they had an intuition that the longing of their soul could be met in the Church. Some of them came because that's what the preacher touted.

They came; they met the *Savior* and wow! The preacher was right. They experienced the joy of salvation. They felt when their burdens rolled away. From that moment, they grabbed a zeal to do all that they could for the Savior who met them in their dirt hole, delivered them from a world of sin and signed their ticket for glory. Little did they know however, that waiting in the shadows were holier than thou, religious Christians. Some of these new converts bask in the sunshine for some time before their first jab, but others receive a rude awakening almost immediately.

Some people come from gangs. In the gangs, there is camaraderie. The love they have for each other is not Christ-centered, but each member is willing to lay down his or her life for other members. They know they can depend on each other. Usually, they do not even fear what law enforcement officials can do to them. Even if they have to go to prison, it doesn't bother them. They know they have buddies already there and the ones who are not incarcerated will visit them. But the gang life is dangerous, so they come to the Church for refuge. They expect greater camaraderie, greater love, greater looking out for each other, but too often they are disappointed.

Backstabbing, criticizing, gossiping, vocalizing discontent with the slow growth of others, not supporting others, name calling and much more are sadly part of the make-up of many of today's churches. The former gang member must muddle through all this to maintain connection with the Savior. If you have been wounded in this way this chapter is for you!

Open Wounds

"And one shall say unto him, what are these wounds in thine hands? Then he shall answer, Those with which I was wounded in the house of my friends."
– Zechariah 13:6

Christians will hurt you the most, but they will also love you the most. Many Christians have been hurt by other church members, so you are not alone. I understand how disappointed and hurt you are because you didn't expect this to happen in the Church. Quitting however is not an acceptable option. Some people have been hurt in the Church and they have turned away from the faith altogether. Why?

- Did Christians save them?
- Did Christians die for them?
- Do Christians have a heaven for them?

So, why get angry with God and turn away from Him because of what an insensitive Christian did? They have wounded you, but you can allow the Lord Jesus to treat your wound so you can continue walking on the highway to heaven. Jesus must treat your wound so it can heal. It must be healed because open wounds serve as doorways to the soul.

> *"You are battered from head to foot—covered with bruises, welts, and infected wounds—without any soothing ointments or bandages."*
>
> **– Isaiah 1:6** *(NLT)*

Many Christians are living today with deep, open wounds caused by other Christians. Do you have any wounds today - wounds caused by past relationships - regurgitating memories of hurt someone inflicted on you? As long as these wounds exist, our adversary can put salt in them to hurt and irritate you. Seek healing for your wounds.

*Just like natural wounds,
allow your wounds time to heal.*

Scars may remain after healing, but there has never been a wound too deep, too wide or too critical for God to heal. A scar is different from a wound. A wound is an open, unhealed area, but a scar demonstrates God's awesome power to heal. A scar serves only as a memory of a wound. The wound is no longer there; it was healed. Jesus still has the scars that prove He was wounded at Calvary. So you may still have scars from some former wounds, but they prove that God is a healer.

Divorce & Separation

Most movies have a happy ending. A young couple standing before the altar on the happiest day of their life has utopia saturating every crevice of their being. Just like it happens in the movies, they are going to live together happy for the rest of their lives. They make a commitment to stay married before God, the minister and a whole host of friends and family. Divorce or separation is the farthest thing from their minds. Statistics however, gives this young, care-free couple only a 50 percent chance of survival.

*Over 50 percent of marriages
end in divorce within 5 years!*

Divorce is usually accompanied by costly, vicious battles. Divorcing couples usually suffer deep wounds in the process. Some of these wounds take years to heal and some never heal.

In their introduction, two of my students said they live with their girlfriends, but they will never marry. Both had caught their *"ex"* wives cheating. The deeds of an unfaithful spouse left wounds that just would not mend.

- Don't allow wounds to detour you!
- Don't allow wounds to drive you to question God's faithfulness!
- Don't allow wounds to snatch the crown you are laboring for!
- Don't allow wounds to linger too long before you seek medical (spiritual) attention!

Hidden Wounds

Within the Church, there are doers and there are those who criticize those who are doing. The doers can get so discouraged by the criticism of others; they shut down and recluse to mend their wounds. This may have happened to you. Although you feel safe in the protective wall you've created, reclusion is not healthy. You are a doer! You are a go getter! You were built that way! That's why you see and do what needs to be done when others don't see what needs to be done. For you to sit and do nothing, puts you outside your comfort zone – in unfamiliar waters. This unfamiliar place is an open doorway and renders you vulnerable to Satan's attacks. You are in a dangerous place. I know you have been hurt in the Church, but ask the Lord Jesus to heal you.

A lot of Christians leave a Church because of wounds caused by other members, but it is not spiritually healthy to leave under such conditions. Resolve the issue first – (**Matt 5:23-24**) and allow the wounds to heal. Wounds need to be healed in the environment where they were created. I have seen some Christians come and join our Church and later discovered they had hidden wounds from another Church. When they ran from their former Church under such conditions, they embraced a running spirit. Unless those wounds are healed, they will keep on running because the door to that running spirit is open and the spirit will continue to drive them. I teach that such members should go back to the Church they ran from and settle the matter. I know that if they don't settle the issue, I could preach like Peter on the day of Pentecost or I could council them until I am exhausted, they will still run to another Church at just the smell of discomfort. They will keep running from Church to Church and hardly will they see the *Gates of Pearls*.

If this describes your situation, God can mend, heal and restore you. Be pliable in His hands so He can fashion you just like clay in the hands of a potter.

> *"And the vessel that he made of clay was marred in the hand of the potter: so he made it again another vessel, as seemed good to the potter to make it. Then the word of the LORD came to me, saying, O house of Israel, cannot I do with you as this potter? saith the LORD.* **Behold, as the clay is in the potter's hand, so are ye in mine hand, O house of Israel.**"

> **– Jeremiah 18:4-6**, emphasis is mine

The Wounder

We have addressed the wounded, but how about the wounder? How about the Christian who takes pride in speaking their own mind? They don't care whose feelings get hurt. They'll just open their mouth and tell people what they think without caring about who gets hurt in the process. It doesn't matter if it's the new convert that the pastor has been working diligently to wean off

the fence. They'll just let them have it! Many people have been hurt by such Christians.

> *"But the tongue can no man tame; it is an unruly evil, full of deadly poison."*
> **– James 3:8**

Many Christians carry wounds today caused by another Christian's tongue. Where do you fit today?

- Are you a woundee or a wounder?
- How many Christians have you daggered?
- How many people have been hurt by your loose words?
- How many people have left the Church because of your uncaring attitude?

Sadly, too many Christians fall into the wounder's category and you know some of them. Regretfully, they do not know this about themselves. Don't you dare try to show them the error of their ways either! They'll snap your head off and chew you up, yet argue that they don't have a bad attitude. Pray that God will open their eyes. Jesus said in **Matthew 18:7** –

> *"Woe unto the world because of offences! For it must needs be that offences come; but woe to that man by whom the offence cometh!"*

Misunderstanding will arise, but we must be cognizant of this and be careful not to cause another Christian to fall by offending them by our words or by our attitudes.

> *"With all lowliness and meekness, with longsuffering, forbearing one another in love; endeavoring to keep the unity of the Spirit in the bond of peace.*

There is one body, and one Spirit, even as ye are called in one hope of your calling."

– **Ephesians 4:2-4**, emphasis is mine

Unity – A Healing Balm

There is power in unity. Unity breaks the cycle of wounding in any institution. Unity frustrates our enemy; that's why he tries to separate us. He instigates the wounder to wound others, and then he instigates the woundee to retaliate or recluse to nurse bitterness and un-forgiveness. This way, he gets two for the price of one, but unity annuls his agenda. Unity is Godly as seen in the eternal unity between Father, Son and Holy Spirit. In **John 17**, Jesus prayed that we may also be one with Him and the Father.

God loves unity.

I questioned you earlier regarding your category. That is, whether you are the woundee or the wounder. Whatever category we fall into, it is critical that we endeavor to keep unity. We are all pilgrims on the journey to the Gates of Pearls. Our chances of getting there significantly improve when we unite. Isolated Christians are easy targets for snipers. So, even if you have been wounded:

- *Pursue unity* with inflexible passion.
- *Pursue unity* with unprecedented fervor.
- *Pursue unity* with excitement and determination.
- *Pursue unity* until hell shakes when you speak.
- *Pursue unity* until your Church is filled with it.

Unity is not only powerful, unity is graceful.

Unity allows God to take the broken fabric of our lives and blend them to create a mosaic of unprecedented artwork. Separately, our rough edges protrude, our weak areas are exposed and our vulnerabilities limit us. But united, we present a concert of matchless harmony and elegance to the world. Look at the separate parts of the choir:

- **Base** – meaning *bottom, foot, pedestal or foundation*.
- **Tenor** – meaning *mood, tone, sense or theme*.
- **Soprano** – meaning *high pitch, piercing, sharp or penetrating*.
- **Alto** – meaning *counter tenor or the second highest voice*.

Individually, these have little or no melody, but together they sooth the ear. They can set the mood; they can even make you so happy that you cry. The melody of a choir is the sum of all the individual pieces. A choir is not all base, not all altos, not all tenors; neither is it all sopranos. It is the sum of all of them. If one member of the tenor is weak, the whole is not necessarily affected because the others make up for the minor imperfection.

As a child, I didn't know any better, so when Aunt Yellow *(not her real name)* sang, in my childhood expression, I would laugh and tell her that her singing didn't have any sugar. She knew this as well, but in her sense of humor, she would join in the laughter. But Aunt Yellow always sang in the church choir. She was always a dedicated member. Her tune, sugarless and uninspiring as it was, always blended in and made the choir a beautiful ensemble.

Isn't it interesting then, that a choir is almost synonymous with the Church? The two are almost inseparable. And it does not end there. When the Church – the redeemed from all ages, pass through the *Gates of Pearls* into glory, angels will sit in quiet awe as we blend together and sing songs of redemption. The Church will form one great choir in heaven. With all our individualities, some tasteless and uninspiring, but the melody of our singing will surpass all human intelligence and will most certainly tempt our tearful emotions. I know I'm going to tear up when we sing *"Holy, Holy, Holy, Lord God Almighty."* Thank God we won't have to sing **Fanny J. Crosby's** *"Near the Cross"* because that just brings me to tears when we sing it down here.

Forgiveness – An Antidote

"And when ye stand praying, forgive, if ye have ought against any: that your Father also which is in heaven may forgive you your trespasses."

– Mark 11:25

So, you have been wounded...

To see the *Gates of Pearls* however, you must forgive everyone, even the Christian who wounded you. As long as the distasteful past event remains stuck in your memory cells, you will be inclined to respond or to get even. The person that wounded you still sits on the choir, so you see them every Sunday. You wish they would change their seat so you wouldn't have to see them while you are trying to focus on what the preacher is saying. You are reminded of the repulsive event every time you see them, but you must forgive them especially since you always ask God to forgive you as you forgive others.

"And forgive us our debts, as we forgive our debtors."

– Matthew 6:12

This shows that sometimes answers to our prayers are hindered because of unforgiveness in our hearts. Notice that Jesus reiterated this concept after He taught the disciples how to pray

"For if ye forgive men their trespasses, your heavenly Father will also forgive you."

– Matthew 6:14

Our own forgiveness is therefore linked to our forgiveness of others. It doesn't matter how spiritual we feel, how many times a day we pray or how often we fast. It doesn't matter how sanctified we believe we are. If we don't forgive those who hurt us, God will not forgive us.

"But if ye forgive not men their trespasses, neither will your Father forgive your trespasses."

– Matthew 6:15

The simple act of unforgiveness can therefore negate all that we do to exhibit righteous lifestyles. God links His forgiveness of our trespasses with our forgiveness of others. Every aspect of our lives may depict good, Christian morals. Everyone who knows us may regard us very highly. If however, someone has done us wrong and we don't forgive them, we won't make it to the *Gates of Pearls* because of that one act of unforgiveness. This is sad!

These are heavens' rules in reference to forgiveness while we are here on earth. Stephen knew them, so just before he died, he forgave those who were stoning him.

> *"And he kneeled down, and cried with a loud voice, Lord, lay not this sin to their charge. And when he had said this, he fell asleep."*

– Acts 7:60

Jesus, the Lord of Glory, while He was on the cross, demonstrated heavens rules on forgiveness as well. Jesus said:

> *"Father, forgive them, they don't know what they are doing."*

– Luke 23:34 *(NLT)*

How To...

Please Sir! Please Ma'am! I beg you with every fiber of my being. If you have left a Church or a relationship because someone did you wrong, please forgive them. This is priceless information and I'm sure you will come looking for me to thank me when you pass through the gates. When you breathe your last breath your destiny is set and you cannot change anything then. Please make things right before the sun goes down today. Tomorrow is promised to no one! Your soul is priceless. Don't let what someone did to you cause you to lose your soul.

We must live in unity down here if we're to join the redeem choir up there. From here on, let's look for wounded soldiers; especially those who have been wounded by friendly fire. Let's nurse their wounds. Let's unite!

Do you have any wounds that need healing? Jesus is able and willing to heal all of them. You may have been carrying them silently for years. Only you know the pain, the worry, the anger or the bitterness that lies beneath the surface because of them. I believe that I have stressed enough that although you may have been wounded even in the house of your friends, a greater part of the healing process may rest in your hands. Often, the key to your healing rests on your shoulders, not the wounder's!

> *"And **make straight paths for your feet**, lest that which is lame be turned out of the way; but let it rather be healed."*
>
> – **Hebrews 12:13-16** emphasis is mine

- Jesus wants to heal you now of all your wounds, but you must first forgive others – Forgive the Wounder!
- Unwillingness to forgive will tie the Savior's hands. Untie His hands.

Forgiveness is not easy but when you ask Holy Spirit to help you to forgive others, He will help you. The next time you see the person who wronged you, anger may begin to rise. Ask *Holy Spirit* to help you every time this happens. Also, every time you remember the event, tell your mind not to receive it. If you still have trouble forgiving, ask *Holy Spirit* again as well.

God is not asking us to do more than He does.

Regardless of all our sins; when we come to the cross, confess our sins and ask for forgiveness, God forgives us of all of them.

Allow *Holy Spirit* to search your heart – whether you a woundee or a wounder!

Jesus wants to heal you, but you have to ask Him to heal you. **Just ask Him.**

God Bless You!

MY PERSONAL THOUGHTS & INSPIRATIONS

CHAPTER 10
HOLY SPIRIT ORCHESTRATED REVIVAL

No doubt, the road to the Gates of Pearls begins at Calvary. Our ticket must have "Calvary" stamped on it. Calvary is the place where we repent of our sins and receive cleansing in Jesus' blood. Christians splinter off into denominational groups after, but as long as our ticket says *"Calvary,"* we are on our way to the *Gates of Pearls*. Calvary however, is only the beginning.

> *"Therefore let us move beyond the elementary teachings about Christ and be taken forward to maturity, not laying again the foundation of repentance from acts that lead to death and of faith in God."*
> – **Hebrews 6:1** *(NLT)*

The subject of the *Holy Spirit's* baptism continues to be a great divide in the twenty-first century Church. In many circumstances, silence has overridden debate or discussion on the subject. Even today, children and grand-children of those who experienced the great 50s & 60s revivals have strayed from their roots and have embraced a more palatable midstream religious culture. Unfortunately, this generational straying is a cycle which is normal in human behavior. We saw it all through the Old Testament where Israel would grow negligent in piety and would walk farther and farther away from God until He administered judgment. Then a prophet or a king would rise to lead them back to God. Restoration or revival would occur, but often only while that prophet or king lived. Sometimes the spiritual renewal the revivalist spearheaded would extend through their children's or grand children's generation, but inevitably, pride and self interest would rebound in the culture. Backsliding would ensue and moral decay would accelerate until judgment, then another leader would rise to affect spiritual revival again.

Solomon said in **Ecclesiastes 1:9**, *"There is nothing new under the sun."* The Church has seen the same roller coaster trend that Israel experienced. From its inauguration on the day of Pentecost, the Church experienced the grandeur of its beginning, then grave persecution by Jewish leaders and then by Roman officials. However, the church's growth steadily continued until it saturated the entire world. But the nagging, daunting, poisoning cycle eventually set in. Holiness, piety and Christ centered Christianity declined until the Church fell into the dark ages.

For over a thousand years, the Church stayed in the dark ages where its existence was bleak and docile. Around the turn of the sixteenth century however, *Holy Spirit* blew a fresh wind into the Church. *Martin Luther*, a Catholic Monk was intrigued while reading his Bible and stumbled across *"The just shall live by faith."* After much prayer, study, meditation, and comparison of justification by faith with what he had been taught, he documented ninety-five things that were not true in the Catholic teachings on justification. He was one of the first of many whom *Holy Spirit* led to study God's word and experienced a spiritual revival. The Holy Spirit revival of Martin Luther's era spread like wild fire across the Western world. People experienced the Holy Ghost baptism and spoke with other tongues just like on the day of Pentecost. During

meetings, they rolled on the floor, hollered and displayed other strange demonstrations, yet their numbers grew rapidly. The revival of the Church in this manner gave rise to the protestant Church. The significant revival of the Church at that time is known as the reformation period. The inevitable lull however, re-emerged and remained until the pendulum swung again just after the turn of the 19th century.

In 1906 *William Seymour*, an African American pastor from Louisiana, traveled to Los Angeles, but was locked out of the Church by the congregation that had sent for him. Why? Glossolalia - speaking in tongues. Seymour turned to prayer and teaching the reality of the baptism of the Holy Spirit. The Azusa Street revival was the result. This revival shook the Church in an unprecedented way. It crossed numerous denominational barriers and changed the lives of over six hundred million people. Almost all of today's Pentecostals can trace their roots back to the Azusa Street revival. By the turn of the twentieth century however, the pendulum swung the other direction and with it, Christian piety and Spirit filled living.

Whatever led the Church into dormancy throughout various periods in history is certainly pulling the Church that way again. Many churches have reached their zenith in membership and some are experiencing decline. Many of them are spiritually cold and lifeless and some are even closing their doors. We face a dire need for revival. We must awake and seek God's face for it!

Holy Spirit's Baptism

The Holy Ghost baptism and speaking in tongues; is it authentic? Is it from God, or is it from the devil? Is it a genuine part of Christianity, or is it just the practice of some Pentecostal fanatics? What tools are we using to evaluate its authenticity? So, what is this Holy Spirit's baptism anyway?

Almost all Christians believe in the doctrine of the **Holy Trinity.** We know that the Church officially started on the day of Pentecost when, as promised by the Lord Jesus, Holy Spirit came like a rushing mighty wind.

> *"All of them were filled with the Holy Spirit and began to speak in other tongues as the Spirit enabled them."*

– **Acts 2:4** *(NIV)*

Church history also shows that authentic revival is never without this speaking in tongues and other emotional expressions. Yet, this charismatic behavior has caused heated arguments and divisions in the Church just as it did on the day of Pentecost. There, the people accused the apostles of being drunk.

So, is this speaking in tongues and the associated unseemly behavior a divine act? Is it just a display of human emotions? Is it ungodly? Every Christian should know that our adversary strives against everything that God orchestrates. We should know also that anything God authenticates will accent Christian behavior while satanic devices and actions will not.

They didn't call the original Protestants Holy Rollers for nothing. They were expressive; they were screamers; and they were emotional. For three days, people from all backgrounds were heard shouting, singing, moaning and speaking in tongues at Azusa Street. They shouted until the foundation of the house gave way.

As people sought out the Azusa street meetings, they fell under the power of God from many blocks away. Emotion was the human expression of God's power. As people came in the meeting house, they would fall under God's power. Proud, well dressed preachers would soon be convicted, then fall and wallow on the floor asking God for forgiveness and humility.

Not only does this behavior look strange, it is eccentric. It is unlike anything we see in our well structured, well timed, order of service in today's Church. When last have you seen this type of expression even in a Pentecostal Church? In the Azusa Street Church, there was no bulleting listing the order of service. Seemingly, there was no structure at all in the meetings, but God moved mightily. There was no choir but people sang for hours. Often, the pastor would only read a scripture. Then, most of the time people moaned, yelled or rolled on the floor. There was not even a time set aside for receiving offering. A basket was set at the door for people who wanted to give.

By our post modern standards, this Church was disorganized, but the very atmosphere demonstrated a great move of God. The people He used and the circumstances also showed consistency in His Word. **1 Corinthians 1:27** *(ASV)* says:

> *"...but God chose the foolish things of the world, that He might put to shame them that are wise; and God chose the weak things of the world, that He might put to shame the things that are strong."*

While Jesus was here on earth, He followed the Father's footsteps also. The men He chose were not men of reputable character. In fact, their extraordinary ability on the day of Pentecost stunned Jerusalem. People described them as unlearned men, yet these uneducated men turned the world upside down. Through them, *Holy Spirit* changed the course of history.

Has God Changed?

Azusa Street shows that He has not changed. William Seymour was the son of African American slaves. In 1906, segregation was very much alive in America, yet churches were well organized and attendance was high. Did God use the 1906 renowned church establishments to revamp revival? Did He solicit the rich, affluent plantation owners? Will He use our well structured churches to launch the next revival? As we look at the characteristics of the Church of Laodicea which represents the last Church Age, we see the Lord addressing individuals rather than the corporate Church. Some may look down on those who pursue and give themselves to the charismatic behavior, but we can all agree that the 1906 revival was authentic – that it came from God. Are we satisfied with the spiritual health of our Church Age? Isn't there a desperate need for revival today? Too often, the human element, human ability and secular worship permeate the atmosphere of today's churches while Holy Spirit orchestrated demonstrations are not present.

As a whole, today's Church is not all that healthy. We have tried to incite revival, but we have not been very successful. Remember the cycle we talked about earlier? Well, it's time for the pendulum to swing our way again. It's time for revival. Especially during this economic down-swing, congregations in the USA are declining and many pastors are experiencing depression or burnout. With all the modern technology and mega congregations, our Church Age is in dire need of revival.

Revival does not depend on man's preferences.

Although conditions are grim, many Christians are privately seeking for that greater anointing; that greater outpouring; that true revival their parents and grandparents experienced. As history shows, revival does not happen through secular efforts, or mere human ability. Revival does not even depend on man's preferences. Revival happens as Christians humble themselves before God, lay aside all human wisdom, and intercede for the souls of men. Don't think then, that the next *Holy Spirit's* revival will be any different from past revivals. We may experience great moves of God in various areas, but until we see the same things that depict authentic revival people falling under God's power, rolling on the floor even in their Sunday best attire, crying out to God in earnest repentance and thousands being saved, we cannot say that we have experienced revival. The *Azusa Street revival* illustrated the essence of *Holy Spirit's* baptism and a consequent revival. Are we ready for this baptism?

> *"The circumcised believers who had come with Peter were astonished that the gift of the Holy Spirit had been poured out even on the Gentiles.* **For they heard them speaking in tongues and praising God**. *Then Peter said, "Can anyone keep these people from being baptized with water?* **They have received the Holy Spirit just as we have**.*"*
>
> – **Acts 10:45-47** *(NIV)* emphasis is mine

Outpouring

The outpouring is a common description of the *Holy Spirit* baptism. The term outpouring depicts an unbiased giver. A consistent indicator of *Holy Spirit's* outpouring is the total disregard for race, ethnicity or financial status. The term outpouring also suggests giv-

ing without measure. With Holy Spirit's outpouring then, God pours out and man becomes so filled with the Spirit of God, man does not have enough room to receive all that is poured in and over him. In a Holy Spirit's revival, man is not doing the pouring, God is! In a Holy Spirit's revival, man's ability diminishes and everyone knows that God is doing the pouring.

> *"And it shall come to pass in the last days, saith God; I will pour out of my Spirit upon all flesh: and your sons and your daughters shall prophesy, and your young men shall see visions, and your old men shall dream dreams."*
>
> – **Acts 2:17**

In revivals, God does more than just fill people with *His Spirit*. Numerous signs and miracles also accompany the *Holy Spirit's* outpouring. At Azusa Street, there were reports of the blind having their sight restored and diseases cured. Uneducated black Christians ministered to German, Yiddish and Spanish speaking immigrants in their native language. This should not surprise us. It was a just replica of events that occurred on the day of Pentecost when *Holy Spirit* first came. We should not be surprised then that He still operates the same way two thousand years later.

Baptism of the Holy Spirit/Holy Ghost Infilling

Holy Spirit's baptism and the ensuing Spirit filled life is not a special, deluxe edition of Christianity. It is all part of the total plan that Jesus set up for His body – the Church. Regeneration and

Holy Spirit's baptism are two separate works of salvation which can occur simultaneously or separately. We don't hear this taught much today, but just a generation ago, those who experienced the great revivals of the 50s, 60s and the 70s taught it. *Acceptance of Christ is a prerequisite for heaven*, but people backslide after accepting Christ. Holy Ghost filled Christians backslide as well, but *Holy Spirit's* baptism forms a greater seal for seeing the *Gates of Pearls*. Jesus said that when He *(Holy Spirit / Spirit of truth)* comes, He would guide us into all truth. The Spirit filled believer then, is a **Spirit led believer**.

> "Holy Spirit knows all things– even the deep things of God."
>
> **– 1 Corinthians 2:1**

He is the only one who knows the way to the *Gates of Pearls*. Wouldn't you want to be Spirit filled and Spirit led then?

> "For as many as are led by the Spirit of God, they are the sons of God."
>
> **– Romans 8:14**

The Church has been around for over two thousand years, yet many Christians today do not know about the baptism of the *Holy Spirit*. The Holy Ghost fire baptism inaugurated the Church, yet many Christians today argue against it and debate its demonstrations. Many reject and strip it from their doctrine as well. Satan has run a relatively successful campaign against this foundation element of the Church. He has fought against it more viciously than any other doctrine of the Church. **Why is this?** Spirit filled Christians offer the greatest resistance to him, so he has interjected fear, confusion, and even sarcasm around the *Holy Spirit* baptism to divide the Church. Yet, Holy Spirit is still working the same way He has always worked. He is still filling people of all color, race and status. If you'd like Him to do the same for you, He will.

In **Acts 19:2**, Paul met Christians in Ephesus and asked them:

> *"Have ye received the Holy Ghost since ye believed? And they said unto him, We have not so much as heard whether there be any Holy Ghost."*

This shows that in the *New Testament Church*, those who spearheaded the Christian movement expected all believers to be filled with Holy Spirit. Yet, these believers had not heard about the infilling so they had not experienced it. Paul baptized them, laid his hands on them and they received Holy Spirit's baptism and spoke in tongues. Holy Spirit's baptism was therefore the norm in the New Testament Church.

From this, we can deduce that when we accept the **Lord Jesus Christ** as *our Savior*, we are eligible to receive this same baptism. In many revivals over the years, as people came with open hearts to meetings where people were being filled, they also received the same Holy Spirit's baptism and spoke in tongues. Often, the usual accompanying persecution occurred as well. Many of them were handed grave rebuke and ridicule from their organized, traditional, religious organization. Some of them were even excommunicated. If you are yet to experience the baptism, don't be surprised if this happens to you also when you do. If that's the worst that happens, just shrug your shoulder and enjoy the infilling. Hey, people in the Middle East are being beheaded just for accepting Christ, yet they are coming to Him by the millions. So what is a little criticism or rebuke for being filled with *Holy Spirit*?

Experiencing Holy Spirit's Baptism

When it comes to spiritual matters, I am adamant about challenging people to have their own personal encounter with God. Holy Spirit's baptism is no less the same. If you are looking for three easy ways to receive the baptism this is not the book. If you are looking for teaching on how to speak in tongues this is not the book either. Holy Spirit has to do the baptizing. He has to fill you with Himself until what He pours in you overflows. ***He is not going to force Himself on you.*** *You must surrender to Him.* **You must ask Him to fill you.**

Holy Spirit is a person who wants to meet you personally. I'm sure if you are serious about experiencing His baptism you will seek until you experience it. It is real! It is genuine!

> *"And be not drunk with wine, wherein is excess; but be filled with the Spirit."*
>
> – **Ephesians 5:18**

Don't seek tongues; seek to be baptized with *Holy Spirit*. If you are a Christian you already know Holy Spirit, so just ask Him to fill you. Cheap things aren't good and good things aren't cheap, so don't be frustrated if you don't experience it right away. People came from as far as China to experience the Azusa Street revival.

Cleanse, Tarry, Wait...

Often, *Holy Spirit's* baptism is not as easy as just asking Holy Spirit to fill you. He fills but He doesn't add. Often, He has to do much cleaning and emptying before He fills. Asking begins the process, but He will not compromise. He will challenge you to rid yourself of any sin, self centeredness, or anything He sees that you need to address first. If you allow Him, He will remove them, but be prepared to experience pain as He does His cleansing. He does not always use anesthesia while He is performing surgery. Remember those people of class who rolled on the dirty floor at Azusa Street? He filled them after removing all their pride. Don't even bother to ask Him to fill you if you are not willing to let go of pride, prejudice, unforgiveness or anything He highlights. Some people call this period of cleansing, tarrying or waiting, but you'll find that we are not waiting on Him; He is waiting on us.

> *"And ye shall seek me, and find me, when ye shall search for me with all your heart."*

– Jeremiah 29:13

Now! Are you sure you want to be filled with God's Spirit? *Holy Spirit* is pure, gentle, truth, the essence of Christ Himself and a comforter, but are you sure you want Him to possess you? Are you sure you are willing to give Him complete control of your life? That's really what it is all about! He is wisdom personified, the breath of God, the love of God and the gentleness of God. Are you sure you want to be possessed by such a person – a person who will accept nothing less than obedience to God's word? Are you willing to surrender self confidence, self motivation, self admiration and self enhancement and be placed on a platform that opposes the world? If you answered yes, then you are ready!

Say,

> *"Father I thank you for the gift of the Holy Spirit. I thank you also for washing me in the blood of Jesus and saving me. Holy Spirit I open my mind, my spirit and my soul to you. Fill me now with all*

of you. If you desire to speak in tongues through my lips, I offer them to you!"

Thank You for baptizing me!

Now, live a spirit filled life, especially as the pendulum swings our way again with revival in its arms.

How To...

- Take time to humble yourself before God and listen to His voice.

- Understand that today's cultural views do not align with God's principles. Develop a closer relationship with God so He can show you the difference between them.

- Be careful not to be critical of the charismatic expressive congregations. We saw that authentic revival is not without charismatic behavior.
- Don't seek tongues. Seek to be filled with Holy Spirit, and then live the spirit filled life.

- Pray for revival. Present yourself to God so He can start the revival in you. Schedule time for prayer, fasting and humbling yourself before God.

– After Jesus was baptized, *Holy Spirit* came in the form of a dove and rested on Him.

– Then Jesus went into the wilderness and fasted forty days and nights.

- Even after we are filled, we should fast as well.

- Let go of everything *Holy Spirit* asks you to give up.

- Be part of a Bible believing ministry.

- Attend church regularly and don't entertain excuses for not going.

- Read **God's word** and always obey *Holy Spirit's* leading.

- *Holy Spirit* knows the way to the *Gates of Pearls*. Allow Him to lead you home.

MY PERSONAL THOUGHTS & INSPIRATIONS

_____

_____

_____

_____

_____

_____

_____

CHAPTER 11
HOLINESS HIGHWAY

We're about to take a sharp turn off *Comfort Highway* onto **Holiness Highway**. Many Christians are indecisive here, but the GPS instructs us to take this turn. Heaven's lights shine through the Gates of Pearls all the way down Holiness Highway. Some are not willing to take this sharp turn because the lighting on Holiness Highway is extremely bright–so bright, it exposes all our little flaws. This exposing of flaws is visible from Comfort Highway, so rather than preparing to address the necessary personal changes, some Christians continue on Comfort Highway to only God knows where. But come with me. We're going the designated route. Holiness Highway is not as crowded as Comfort Highway, so we'll have enough room to make the necessary adjustments and speed on our journey.

> *"Dearest friends, when I was there with you, you were always so careful to follow my instructions. And now that I am away you must be even more careful to do the good things that result from being saved, obeying God with deep reverence, shrinking back from all that might displease Him."*
>
> **– Philippians 2:12** *(TLB)*

Holiness is an absolute necessity for entrance to heaven and the Bible is the only book on holiness. I can only reiterate its guidelines and stress the importance of avoiding the things that would render us as not holy. In **Genesis 17:1** God told Abram:

> *"I am the Almighty God; walk before me, and be thou perfect."*

Holiness is the attainment of perfection. **James 2:23** says:

> *"And the scripture was fulfilled which saith, Abraham believed God, and it was imputed unto him for righteousness: and he was called the Friend of God."*

The Lord Jesus is the righteousness of God and we are the righteousness of God in Him, **2 Corinthians 5:21** & **Romans 3:22**. Through Christ therefore, we have obtained perfection. We are –

> *"a chosen generation, a royal priesthood, a holy nation, a peculiar people."*

– 1 Peter 2:9

God did all this for us, but maintaining this status is left to us. Christianity is a partnership between God and man. There is a part for God and a part for us. God always does His part – we have to do ours.

Holiness rests on the foundation of integrity.

Indeed, we encounter difficulties, trials and pressures from various areas of today's culture. Integrity however, must guide us

and dictate our daily decisions. It is commendable when we have a reputation of integrity, but our private lives must also exemplify the same. We are accountable to Holy Spirit first. He sees and knows everything we do, so we must observe and embrace integrity in our private lives just as much as in the public's view. Joseph illustrated this in **Genesis 39:9** when he was drawn into a private place with Potifar's wife.

Book on Holiness?

The *Mosaic Law* made people aware of their sins, but it lacked the power to deliver them from sin. This proves that details for holy living are not necessarily documented in a rule book. God gave Israel the Law – the *Ten Commandments*, yet they missed it altogether. If you are looking for a set of do's and don'ts to live holy, you've missed it as well. **1 Samuel 16:7** *(NIV)* says:

> *"The LORD does not look at the things people look at. People look at the outward appearance, but the LORD looks at the heart."*

Holiness begins in the heart.

You don't follow a list of rules to reach holiness status. The way you live is a result of being holy. Holiness is living the way God wants us to live instead of the way we think we should live.

If you are looking for guidelines on living holy look in God's word. I can share some things that constitute anti-holiness; yet the absence of these in your life does not necessarily constitute holiness. I cannot stress enough the importance of seeking truth through God's word and listening to Holy Spirit. Holy Spirit lives here. He came to earth on the day of Pentecost and has not left since. Jesus said He will guide us into all truth, so just listen to Him and obey Him.

> *"And ye need not that any man teach you: but as the same anointing teacheth you of all things, and is truth."*

– I John 2:27

Total Surrender

This is what it will cost you to get to the *Gates of Pearls*. It will cost you your life! It will cost you the total surrendering of your will and much sacrifice. Holiness is the acquisition of the mind where nothing is more important than pleasing God. Be prepared to give up your rights, your hopes, your dreams and your ambitions. You must be prepared to deny yourself many earthly desires if you're to walk through the gates to the holy city of God. Everything Jesus did, He did to please God. To follow Him we must do the same:

> *"And he said to them all, If any man will come after me, let him deny himself, and take up his cross daily, and follow me."*

– Luke 9:23

This area of surrender is not popular with many Western Christians because it is not the structure in our free, equal rights,

democratic, capitalist culture. For example: this surrendering requirement will not sit well today with many women because it asks them to submit to their husband. **Ephesians 5:22** –

> *"Wives, submit yourselves unto your own husbands, as unto the Lord."*

Women have suffered greatly over the centuries and regretfully, this abuse continues even today. God's directives do not even remotely propagate abuse of women. Along with other social institutions, the women's liberation movement has led the way in heightening awareness of this problem. Legislative response to this awareness has curbed much domestic abuse. The old adage however, is applicable here. *"Two wrongs don't make one right."* Some women have retaliated so much, they are now manipulating and abusing men. Male pastors in one New York organization complained that their wives threaten to withhold sexual intimacy if they don't comply with their demands for leadership roles in the Church. These women get their way, but the *Word of God* commands women to submit to their husbands.

> *"Be beautiful inside, in your hearts, with the lasting charm of a gentle and quiet spirit that is so precious to God. That kind of deep beauty was seen in the saintly women of old, who trusted God and fitted in with their husbands' plans."*
>
> – **1 Peter 3:4-5** *(TLB)*

It doesn't matter what position you hold in the Church. You could be the pastor, the esteemed First Lady or the bishop. If you do not submit to your husband, there is no way you'll see the *Gates of Pearls*. Check with *Holy Spirit* if you don't believe me. I am not even remotely suggesting that your husband should usurp authority over you or abuse you in any way. If he abuses you, he won't see the gates either; even if he is the Archbishop of Bethlehem. He should allow you to fulfill your role as his helper. God intended for it to be this way right from the inception of marriage. God created the woman as a helper for the man. Therefore, if a man is succeeding, check out his help. If he is failing, check out his help as well.

Trust Holy Spirit to help in your marriage.

In God's ideal for marriage, the master-slave or boss-subordinate mentality simply does not exist. The domineering type of personality – and especially the type that engages in any kind of abuse, whether verbal or physical – is demonically influenced, evil, and it should never be tolerated. Each situation is so unique; it would not be wise to lay down a blanket rule for all marital issues. Trust *Holy Spirit* to help you in your marriage relationship. He does not support any type of spousal abuse; so, solicit His wisdom for your particular situation.

Leader's Responsibilities

Don't ever think that God has a gender bias. It was God's prerogative to place the man as the head of the family. We may not like this structure and especially in our post modern culture, many may not agree with it, but God is sovereign. He is not trying to come to our earth; we are trying to get to His heaven. Heaven is His home and He has every right to set the rules for entrance to His home. It is His prerogative to allow who He allows there. So, I am telling you that He commands husbands to lead their families and

to love their wives as Christ loved the Church. This is an uphill battle for many men today, but husbands must love their wives.

> *"Husbands, love your wives, even as Christ also loved the church, and gave Himself for it."*
>
> – **Ephesians 5:25**

Once again, it doesn't matter if you are the pastor or the senior bishop of the Jerusalem Diocese. If you do not love your wife there is no way you'll make it to heaven either. You may argue that your wife tramples on your last nerve with her Sunday – go – to – meeting high heel shoes, or that she is always ready to fight and argue with you about the decisions you make. I must tell you however, that you must forgive her and love her if you want to walk on the streets of gold. If you think this is too difficult, ask Holy Spirit for help. Read the chapters *"Living in the Lion's Den and Forgiveness"* in my book ***"Thoughts For The Hurting Heart."***

Divorce and remarriage even among the clergy is high.

It is a growing concern since pastors and church leaders are expected to provide council to trouble marriages. If they are having the same marital problems, what kind of council can they provide? The pressure against marriage today is mounting and a lot of church leaders will miss heaven just because of the issues in their marriage. They do not follow the structure that God set up.

IT DOESN'T SEEM FAIR! Satan instigates our spouse and uses them as an instrument to irritate us, tempt us, get on our last nerve or even abuse us. Then, when we retaliate or find it hard to forgive them, he uses our failure to forgive as a legitimate argument against us. Our marriage may be our thorn in the flesh, but God promised not to put more on us than we can bear. In your irritable, nerve racking or abusive situation, God is still saying:

"My grace is sufficient for thee: for my strength is made perfect in weakness."

– 2 Corinthians 12:9

Seek His guidance for your particular situation.

All or Nothing

That's right! Holiness does not compromise. It's all or nothing. A man came to see me in my church office. He told me that his mom raised him in the Church, but he had strayed. Now, in his sixties and becoming more aware of his own mortality, he thought it was time for him to come back to Church. I commended him for taking that step and I shared a few more comments. Then he shocked me. He said: *"I live with a woman, but I have no intention of ever getting married to her."* I almost swallowed my Adam's apple.

After I caught my breath, I struggled for palatable words, but mumbled only a few incoherent phrases. Then, the resolve that drives Eversel Griffith hit me. I said, *"I'm sure you'll find a church within walking distance from here whose pastor will tell you it's okay, but I have to tell you the truth."* Then I asked him, *"Why would you join the Church, pay your tithes and offerings, sing on the choir, do all the things that Christians do, then fail to make*

heaven?" I told him, *"God's word says; without Holiness no man shall see God."* He left my office and never came back.

As I thought about it some months later, I questioned whether I was too blunt; whether I should have allowed him to join the Church and hope that my teaching and preaching would incite a change in him. I reasoned that he knew fornication was an anti-Christian behavior; otherwise he would not have brought up the subject. Most likely, in answer to his long gone mother's prayers, *Holy Spirit* was speaking to him. He had recognized *Holy Spirit's* beckoning. However, he was not willing to change his lifestyle. He wanted only to be justified in his ways. Holiness does not work that way. Holiness demands all or nothing.

We must recognize that there is a distinct difference between holiness and ungodliness. God of the Old Testament did not compromise. He told Saul to kill all the Amalekites including the king and their domestic animals. Has God changed? Is the God of the Old Testament different from the God of the twenty-first century? NO! Jesus came to show the Father's love, but God still demands that we live in the world, but not like the world. He still expects holiness in our lives.

- *God loves* sinners, but He will not excuse sin.
- *God loves* the adulterer, but He will not ignore adultery.
- *God loves* people, but He will not condone abortion.
- *God loves* the homosexual but He will not ignore homosexuality.

Many countries are legalizing homosexuality, but this sin is particularly listed as an abomination *(detestable sin)* **Leviticus 18:22** & **20:13**. This sin resulted in the severing of God's mercy from *Sodom* and *Gomorrah*. That society had become so sinful;

God could not even find ten righteous people there so He could spare it from destruction. Our culture is embracing this alternative lifestyle, but Christians must stay firm on God's principles, knowing the world's culture does not dictate the guidelines of holiness. Christians who back political candidates that support these agendas must also consider where they stand and their destination.

Holiness is decisive. It's all or nothing. The name of the highway to the *Gates of Pearls* is *"Holiness."* If ever so often you don't see a huge billboard sign with megawatt lighting saying *"Holiness Unto The Lord"* or *"Holiness Highway,"* you may have strayed off the highway and onto the wrong one. The road to the *Gates of Pearls* requires absolute holiness in our lives. Holiness demands our undivided attention and commitment to God.

"Love the LORD your God with all your heart and with all your soul and with all your strength."

– **Deuteronomy 6:5** *(NIV)*

Holiness impacts every aspect of our life: what we say, what we do, where we go, what we wear and even our social activities.

In his Epistle, Peter reiterated the importance of holiness in the Christian's life and spoke of God's judgment beginning with the Church. Peter was not very optimistic about the Church's outcome after judgment. He posed a rhetorical question which solidifies his concern for the Church's wellbeing.

"If it is hard for the righteous to be saved, what will become of the ungodly and the sinner?"

– **1 Peter 4:18** *(NIV)*

This is the type of question that cause us to stop whatever we are doing or wherever we are going and evaluate our spiritual coordinates. Is Peter saying that making it to heaven is not as easy as taught by almost every Christian denomination? The Bible even says:

"Believe on the Lord Jesus and thou shall be saved."

Romans 10:9-10 also says:

"If thou shalt confess with thy mouth the Lord Jesus, and shalt believe in thine heart that God hath raised him from the dead, thou shalt be saved."

So, what could Peter be insinuating? Is he contradicting these scriptures?

It is a prevailing ideology in the Christian Church today that if we join the Church we can make it to heaven. From Peter's assessment however, reaching heaven by merely joining a Church cannot be any farther from the truth. Jesus alluded to these misconceived guidelines as well. The *seven kingdom parables* He taught in **Matthew 13** shows a marked difference between the *kingdom of heaven* and *the kingdom of God*. In the kingdom of heaven, the wheat and the tares grow together, but at the appropriate time, He will separate them.

So, joining a Church is commendable, but it will not necessarily enable one to enter heaven. The guidelines for heaven are inflexible. Holiness is an absolute necessity for entrance.

"Follow peace with all men, and holiness, without which no man shall see the Lord."
– **Hebrews 12:14**

- Holiness is a life that is set apart for God.

- Holiness is not Pentecostalism; neither is it speaking in tongues.

- Although holiness influences our dressing, our attire does not necessarily define holiness.

- Holiness is the integrity that God requires of all those who will walk through the *Gates of Pearls*.

- Holiness and worship *(true worship)* are inseparable.

You may wonder why I stressed **true worship**. That's because the type of worship or the ritual of worship that various churches have developed or adopted may not necessarily constitute true worship, or the type of worship that God accepts. To us, the ecumenical order, the tone of singing, the specific action of the presiding minister may be graceful. These rituals can create a solemn atmosphere which may even leave one with a feeling of unearthly venture, but that does not necessarily mean that God accepts the solemn, religious exercise as worship. The essence of true worship is more spiritual than physical or even emotional.

There was an ongoing argument between the Jews and the Samarians regarding the right place to worship. Jesus met a Samarian woman and it didn't take long for her to bring up the subject of geographical worship. **John 4:21** –

> *"Jesus saith unto her, Woman, believe me, the hour cometh, when ye shall neither in this mountain, nor yet at Jerusalem, worship the Father."*

Jesus spoke of the abolition of the whole idea of ceremonial worship and introduced the *New Testament* type. True worship then, as expressed by Jesus is an expression from the heart more so

than from a geographical location. Worship is more about our attitude than ritualistic observances. Worship on Sundays is intended to be the height of an ongoing relationship with Christ. It should be the zenith of our weeklong meditation on God's word and interaction with Jesus.

> *"And they said to one another, Did not our heart burn within us while He talked with us on the road, and while He opened the Scriptures to us?"*
>
> – **Luke 24:32** *(NKJV)*

If you want to see what true worship is you have to look at worship in heaven and visualize.

> *"Day and night they never stop saying: "Holy, holy, holy is the Lord God Almighty, who was, and is, and is to come....the twenty-four elders fall down before Him who sits on the throne and worship Him who lives forever and ever. They lay their crowns before the throne and say: You are worthy, our Lord and God, to receive glory and honor and power, for you created all things, and by your will they were created and have their being."*
>
> – **Revelation 4:8** &**10-11** *(NIV)*

Holiness In The Temple

In the *Old Testament*, God handed down ordinances that constituted true worship. Although they were only temporary, the guidelines for worship were stringent. The High Priest could not just saunter into the Holy of Holies at any time. If he deviated from the prescribed order, he would die as soon as he entered the Holy of Holies. There could not be any deviation from the prescribed order. God accepted only holy, specific worship.

In the *New Testament*, Jesus came and fulfilled the law by offering the ultimate sacrifice. Does this mean that the serenity and sanctity of worship is no longer necessary? Absolutely not! God still requires holiness ingrained in worship.

> *"God is a Spirit: and they that worship Him must worship Him in spirit and in truth."*

– John 4:24

This *New Testament* type of worship must originate from the heart. Holiness originates from the heart as well. God required holiness in the temple worship. We are now His temple and He requires the same from us.

> *"...For we are the temple of the living God. As God has said: "I will live with them and walk among them, and I will be their God, and they will be my people."*

– 2 Corinthians 6:16 *(NIV)*

In the books of **Jeremiah** and *Ezekiel* God expressed that the people worshipped Him with their lips, but not from their hearts. Jesus ridiculed the religious practices of His day as well; often expressing disgust with the manmade traditional worship. If Jesus evaluated that the worship His fellow Jews offered was repulsive, obviously, the Father didn't accept it either. True *(acceptable)* worship ascends to God's throne only from people who are leading holy lifestyles. A holy lifestyle is not only a requirement for acceptable worship; it is also a prerequisite for entrance to heaven.

The road of holiness is not easy, but it's not impossible. We live in a post modern society where technology is unprecedented, but God has not changed. The holiness He required of any other generation, He requires of us as well. It is absolutely all right with God if we want to follow a religion that was developed by someone who claims to be enlightened. To cross the finish line however, we must embrace the truth of God's word alone.

A Right Way

In his letter, Peter insinuated that the criteria for heaven are so stringent, even people who many consider as righteous, will scarcely be saved. In **Mark 10:25-27** Jesus said:

> *"It is easier for a camel to go through the eye of a needle, than for a rich man to enter into the kingdom of God. And they were astonished out of measure, saying among themselves, who then can be saved?"*

- Are you sure God sanctions your religious beliefs?
- Are you sure God will accept the lifestyle you've lived?
- Will holiness be stamped on your efforts for heaven?
- Will holiness be stamped on your life?

God is revealing much information to the Church today regarding the narrowness of the way to heaven. Every day, more and more people are sharing revelations of heaven and the strict guidelines for getting there. Many Christians treat these revelations with callousness and unbelief. A good number of those who stand on the theologically educated platform do not believe these testimonies at all, because such revelations do not align with much of their theological ideologies. However, there can only be one right way to heaven. Either this group of theologians is right and those who claim to have received revelations of heaven are wrong, or the theologians are wrong and these revelations are authentic.

My inclination is to believe many of the revelations of the criteria for heaven, especially since they relate closely to what the Lord Jesus showed me in a dream almost thirty years ago. *(See my book "Thoughts From His Heart")* Also, *Holy Spirit* validates these revelations.

> *"For as many as are led by the Spirit of God, these are sons of God."*

– Romans 8:14

In the book of **Revelation**, the Lord Jesus reiterated to all of the seven churches:

> *"Let him that hath an ear hear what the spirit says to the church."*

We should always listen to *Holy Spirit*. He knows the way to the *Gates of Pearls*. Today, Holy Spirit is saying to the Church that its age is ending soon. He is encouraging us to consider our beliefs and religious practices, be prepared to drop them if necessary, and search for the right way to heaven. As you saw in earlier chapters, you could possibly be committing sins *(by omission or commission)* which could prevent you from crossing the finish line and *"I didn't know"* won't be an acceptable excuse.

In **Matthew 7:22-23** Jesus said:

> *"Many will say to me in that day, Lord, Lord, have we not prophesied in thy name? And in thy name have cast out devils? And in thy name done many wonderful works? And then will I profess unto them, I never knew you: depart from me, ye that work iniquity."*

Can you imagine how disappointing, shocking and heartbreaking it will be for world renowned preachers or miracle workers to hear Jesus say *"I never knew you"*? If Jesus never knew the miracle workers or great preachers, where do we stand? Indeed, they worked many miracles or rather, Jesus did many miracles through them, but their private lives did not align with the guidelines of holiness. Not even miracles then are prerequisites for heaven. HOLINESS IS!

Pastor Jack

Pastor Jack *(not his real name)*: A ministerial trainer; praying, reading and studying God's word from 4 AM until late at night, seeing great miracles – people being saved, healed and delivered even from witchcraft, just because Pastor Jack and his ministerial team came to their town. Yet, Jesus visited Jack and told him: *"If I had come for the Church today, I wouldn't take you."* Jack said the things that seemed small in our eyes seemed incredibly horrid as Jesus addressed them. Jesus showed Jack his life and the reasons why he would have missed the rapture – pride, church politics, lusting after women in his mind and many other things. Jesus reiterated that it is not the miracles, but the holiness that matters. Every time I see this testimony, I search my heart and ask *Holy Spirit* to help me to live holy.

Pastor Jack's testimony shows that it is possible to pray, fast, read the Bible, attend church regularly and still not be eligible to pass through the gates. I'm not talking about backsliding. Many Christians perform all these actions, yet walk around with much bitterness and resentment. They fight and manipulate others in their home, on their job and even in the Church. They must stop this behavior and pursue humility and holiness instead. They must make a total surrender if they're to see the gates.

A Narrow Way

Most Western Christian culture promotes an easy way to heaven, but this can give a false sense of security. Some people join a church with the same mindset as they would when joining a club. They enjoy the fellowship and the social gatherings. Have a concert and the Church has standing room only! As soon as the minister begins to teach or preach on the guidelines of holiness, people find all kinds of excuses to stay away. Jesus experienced this same mindset in His day. As long as He was healing the sick, stretching bread and fish to feed thousands, multitudes followed Him. As soon as He began to talk about the stringent guidelines for heaven the crowds turned away.

Holiness, the way to heaven is not easy, but the fact that others have already been successful in reaching there, confirms that it is possible for us make it. In **Matthew 7:13-14** Jesus told us that *it wouldn't be easy; that the way was narrow. To make it through this narrow path* we must surrender our ideologies, our own understanding, our ideas, our religion, and listen carefully to what *Holy Spirit* is saying.

Peter knew firsthand the narrowness of the way. He thought he had the ego and strong leadership skills to succeed, until he fell flat on his face after Jesus' arrest. As he implies in **1 Peter 4**, many Christians will not reach the *Gates of Pearls* because their lifestyle will not meet God's holy standards. We have a choice today though! We are still on the side of mercy, but we must surrender our wills now to the Lord Jesus Christ and allow Him to judge our thoughts, our actions, our speech and even what we allow our eyes to see.

We must reject the ways of the world and resolve even to suffer if that's what it takes to reach the gates.

> *"Forasmuch then as Christ hath suffered for us in the flesh, arm yourselves likewise with the same mind: for he that hath suffered in the flesh hath ceased from sin."* **– 1 Peter 4:4**

Western Christian culture spurns this suffering aspect of following Christ, but often discomfort is a pertinent part of Christianity's package.

- Are you willing to put aside everything that would blemish a holy life, so you can cross heaven's threshold?
- Are you willing to lead a holy life from this very minute?
- Are you willing to suffer for Christ if that's what it takes to see His smiling face?

There is a proliferation of prosperity preaching in today's Christian culture. There is nothing wrong with seeking a better lifestyle down here, but God challenges us to put a better lifestyle secondary and prioritize holiness. He challenges all gate seekers to put religion, tradition and beliefs second to holiness. It may be that

much of what we consider as holiness does not meet God's standards. Holiness is not our religious activities on Sundays. It's not how we act while we are in a church setting. Holiness is lived seven days a week, twenty-four hours a day and even while we are asleep. We have to reject whatever the devil brings to us even in our dreams. Holiness demands that we daily embrace and follow *Holy Spirit's* directions or convictions. Ensure that you are hearing *Holy Spirit's* voice. He speaks to us about surrendering our will and:

- Being obedient to our pastor.
- Paying our tithes and church attendance.
- Our language and our attire.
- Sharing the gospel with others

In seeking to satisfy the requirements of holiness, it is critical that we develop a meaningful relationship with *Holy Spirit*. He is patient. He is kind, but He won't stick around if we consistently reject Him. Although He lives in us He is yet God. We must obey Him and turn away from the things He convicts of.

"...let us strip off every weight that slows us down, especially the sin that so easily trips us up."

– Hebrews 12:1 *(NLT)*

None of us are perfect; we are growing on to perfection. As we seek God's face, He will show us even the little sins in our lives. As we abandon all our personal goals just to give precedence to God's will, we move closer to holiness as so many others have already done.

- *Enoch* pleased God

"And Enoch walked with God: and he was not; for God took him. **– Genesis 5:24**

- *Shadrach*, *Meshach*, and *Abednego* abandoned self interest to please God instead of the king of Babylon or the ruling authorities.

How To...

The following is not a comprehensive list of things we must do to reach holiness status. In fact, only *Holy Spirit* has an all-inclusive list; that's why I always refer people to Him.

We must practice speaking the truth.

We must pay our tithes. In **Malachi 3:8** *(NLT)* God said:

"Yet you have cheated me! But you ask, 'What do you mean? When did we ever cheat you? "You have cheated me of the tithes and offerings due to me."

We must attend church services, especially prayer and Bible study.

"Not giving up meeting together, as some are in the habit of doing, but encouraging one another — and all the more as you see the day approaching."

– **Hebrews 10:25***(NIV)*

We must not indulge in sexual sins. Don't condone or indulge in anyone's sins either. For example: Some families are committed Christians, yet they allow their daughter's boyfriend or their son's girlfriend to sleep over *(in the same bedroom)*.

Sin – *All sin is the opposite of holiness.*

"If we say that we have no sin, we deceive our-selves, and the truth is not in us."

– 1 John 1:18

It is therefore, critical that we solicit *Holy Spirit's* guidance and obey His instructions whenever He highlights sin in our lives. As you continue on this highway, be honest – be open to change and adjust your habits and practices whenever Holy Spirit points to them. If you do, He will stamp your ticket *"Holiness."* Angels will allow you to enter through the Gates of Pearls when you get there.

God Bless You!

CHAPTER 12
THE VALLEY OF TEMPTATION

The road to the *Gates of Pearls* runs through the valley of temptation. It would be nice if there was an alternate route that heaven bound travelers could use to bypass this gruesome valley. Unfortunately, there is none; everyone must pass through this valley. This valley however, is not prejudice. Everyone is tempted here; the pastor, the deacon, the minister, the evangelist and even the baby Christian who got saved last Sunday. If the devil had the right and the audacity to tempt the Lord Jesus in the wilderness, he has a legitimate right to tempt us as well.

The subject of temptation needs special attention especially since the body of Christ is under severe attack in this area. Church leaders are falling by the dozens through various temptations. Their falling is creating an avalanche in the Church and those whose eyes were fixed on them, are walking away in disappointment and frustration.

As we travel through this valley, always remember that God called us out of darkness into light and that we are now the light of the world. Temptation from various areas looms high in this valley, but God expects us to remain faithful in holiness.

> *"No temptation has overtaken you except what is common to humanity. God is faithful, and*

He will not allow you to be tempted beyond what you are able, but with the temptation, He will also provide a way of escape so that you are able to bear it."

– 1 Corinthians 10:13 *(HCSB)*

Sexual Immorality

Temptation is a ghastly attack that is bombarding the Church. Satan has used this subtle, deceptive tool to detour people since the beginning of time. In these last days, sexual immorality is attacking the Church with unprecedented intensity. Its victims are many and graves are becoming overcrowded. The town through which this highway passes should really be renamed *"Death Valley."* It is proving to be the town where a great number of Christians experience downfalls. As we learn how to resist sexual immorality, we can apply the knowledge we acquire to resist other areas of temptation as well.

Christians should strive ardently against sexual immorality, since so many have backslidden because of its clutches. Although this type of immorality has been historically stamped on men as their area of weakness, women are not innocent either. Adultery is one sin that one cannot commit alone. If you believe you are secure and that you wouldn't be affected by this, beware! Watch and pray! Pray with one eye open! **1 Corinthians 10:12** says:

"Therefore let him who thinks he stands take heed lest he falls."

Behind sexual immorality is a dark, subtle spiritual force that has come against the Church with viciousness and determination.

Sadly, some church leaders have succumbed to its attacks. If this has happened in your Church, you may have a struggle on your hand. You may be committed to holy living, but you must prayerfully and seriously consider whether you should remain in the setting. I explained this to a minister who experienced this in his Church: *"Your pastor is your spiritual covering. If your spiritual covering has been attacked, defeated and tarnished, you are left without the proper covering or protection. This ill-protection increases your vulnerability to the same spirit of immorality that attacked your pastor and caused him or her to fall."*

Some churches have encountered this problem within their leadership. The pastor resigned and they acquired another pastor, but within a few years, the new pastor fell into the same predicament. If the congregation does not acquire a determined, humble, God seeking, spirit filled pastor, the problem will continue there because the former pastor opened a doorway that allowed Satan to gain a foothold in the Church. If the immoral spirit is not dealt with through prayer, fasting and exercising spiritual authority, it's just a matter of time before the members begin to realize the same problem in their lives.

If your Church is struggling with this issue, seriously consider your own spiritual wellbeing. Consider whether you should remain in that environment. You cannot take any chances in this last stretch towards home. Repel anything that has even the slightest inclination to detour you. You must resolve that you are going to reach the gates even without your church friends.

> *"If your hand causes you to sin, cut it off. It is better for you to enter into life maimed, rather than having two hands, to go to hell, into the fire that shall never be quenched."*
> **– Mark 9:43**

Do not be apprehensive in prayer and seeking God's guidance to engage in spiritual warfare against this immoral spirit that is spreading over states and countries. The reality is that evil spirits work diligently to find our vulnerabilities. If they determine that we are weak in the area of sexual immorality, they will arrange people, events or situations that will instigate our passion for sexual gratification. Then, they will begin to attack our minds and wear us down with explicit infatuations. They will prod, poke and push us towards their projected fascination. Knowledge is power, so resist them.

> *"Run from sexual sin! No other sin so clearly affects the body as this one does. For sexual immorality is a sin against your own body."*

– 1 Corinthians 6:18 *(NLT)*

The spirit of immorality will not come to your house, ring your door-bell and ask permission to come in. Like all other evil spirits, this spirit is subtle, deceptive and trespasses. That is why some Christians are falling into sexual misconduct even with other married church members.

Where It Begins

> *"But every man is tempted when he is drawn away of his own lust, and enticed. Then when lust hath conceived, it bringeth forth sin and sin, when it is finished, bringeth forth death."*

– James 1:14-15

All actions start in the mind. Great bridges, skyscrapers, airplanes and trains, all started as a thought in someone's mind. Satan knows the power of the mind. He knows if he can influence the mind, he can control all consequent actions. If you have fallen into sexual immorality, look in retrospect over the details of your predicament and you will realize that the first step towards impropriety started in your mind - a little thought of infatuation. As you yielded to the temptation and opened your mind to those thoughts, your fall began. Since you allowed the little thoughts to linger, our adversary increased his ammunition and bombarded your mind with more intense innuendos and suggestions. Then he lured you into an environment where, as far as you believed, you were just humoring yourself. But those little thoughts you entertained earlier rendered you weak and powerless to resist the enemy's next move. You indulged; you sinned against your own flesh and against God.

Please repent sincerely. This will allow you back into God's presence. You need His presence to help you defeat immorality and put you back on track.

> *"And they overcame him by the blood of the Lamb, and by the word of their testimony; and they loved not their lives unto the death."*
>
> **– Revelation 12:11**

The internet and social media are great tools, but their ease, accessibility and privacy allow them to be a conduit for sexual promiscuity. As we have seen, we're attack first in our mind, so we must use these social tools wisely and not allow our minds to fall to the temptations they offer so blithely. **2 Corinthians 10:4-5** says:

> *"For the weapons of our warfare are not carnal, but mighty through God to the pulling down of strong*

*holds; Casting down **imaginations**, and every **high thing** that exalteth itself against the knowledge of God, and bringing into captivity **every thought** to the obedience of Christ."*

Emphasis is mine

This scripture deals with the mind and our ability in that realm. The battlefield is in the mind so we must fight back in our mind.

To overcome, first take control of your thought life. You have authority to control your thought life. If you don't allow Satan to push his little toe into your thoughts he cannot get the rest of his muscles in to lure you into performing his interjections. In **Philippians 2:5**, Paul encouraged us to embrace Christ's mind to overcome:

"Let this mind be in you, which was also in Christ Jesus."

Focus

When we look at the high profile church leaders who are falling to temptation, we should understand that Satan is touting success record with this tool. He is convinced that since he is able to defeat some of these Christian icons, he can take you down as well. But *"the devil is a liar."* Never mind who is falling – never mind what other church folks are doing; you resist temptation. Don't be overly concerned about the questionable actions of other

Christians either; strive to get to the gates! Jesus stands at the gates with your reward, so focus on Him, not on others.

> *"He that hath an ear, let him hear what the Spirit saith unto the churches. To him that overcometh will I give to eat of the hidden manna, and will give him a white stone, and in the stone a new name written, which no man knoweth saving he that receiveth it."*
>
> **– Revelation 2:17**

Despite the many temptations you encounter, be inflexible. Do not allow them to stop you from achieving your objective. You have all the resources of heaven available to help you overcome. You don't have to fail because others you thought would make it failed. Jesus was also tempted, but He overcame, so keep your eyes on Him.

> *"For we have not an high priest which cannot be touched with the feeling of our infirmities; but was in all points tempted like as we are, yet without sin."*
>
> **– Hebrews 4:15**

Temptations may delay you or even detour you, but keep seeking to get back on the highway to glory. Keep pressing on with the determination to make it to the end. If you have to, struggle relentlessly to overcome all temptations posted on signs along this area of the highway. You may not necessarily win every time or you may not even succeed in the timeframe you had anticipated, but keep working at it. Some issues take time to be resolved. Sometimes, you may be cornered or even weather-bound and may have to wait patiently for the weather conditions to improve. Just keep focusing on the finish line.

"Blessed is the man that endureth temptation: for when he is tried, he shall receive the crown of life, which the Lord hath promised to them that love him."

– James 1:12

The Battle

Prayer is one of the most aggressive and effective ways of fighting back, so expect retaliation from our enemy in this area. When we are praying, distractions bombards our mind from every direction. That's because evil spirits see when our prayers are reaching heaven. They know that if we continue praying we will see answers, so they try various ways to distract us. They solicit other spirits to distract us by bombarding our mind with various thoughts so they can stop us from praying.

You are not aware that all these things are happening in the spirit realm, so the following is a list of some of these distractions, and how they materialize in the natural realm. This insight will better prepare you to fight back:

1. **The telephone rings:** You are sure you'll just answer the phone and return to pray. But often, those spirits ensure that the call requires your immediate attention. Even when you go back to prayer, you can't pick up from where you left off. You have to first fight off the spirits that occupied the heavenly realm while you were distracted. Don't answer the phone.

2. **Pain or Discomfort:** This should be no surprise that evil spirits can afflict our body even during prayer. They specialize in sickness

and disease. God cannot put pain or sickness on us because He doesn't have any of those things up there in heaven. Pain in our knees shows up out of nowhere when we are praying. Our knees are perfectly okay, but they start hurting when we are kneeling. Guess who is causing this? Just rebuke those demons and keep on praying.

3. **Remembering a chore:** Evil spirits bring all kinds of chores you need to do or things you forgot to do, to your mind. They also barrage your mind with various events on your job, things in your family and even issues in the Church. Rebuke them and keep on praying.

4. **Hunger:** This is another distraction, but from here on don't allow the devil to defeat you with this one. You don't have to run to the refrigerator for a glass of milk or to the pantry for cereal. You are not going to die if you miss one meal. Stay on your knees! Maybe, an angel that has the answer to your prayers is about to get through and Satan is desperately trying to distract you so he can legitimately delay the angel.

5. **Others:** The door bell rings, the kids begin to fight or they have a sudden urgent need for cupcakes, the dog barks, the fire alarm goes off and the best one: *"Look at the clock!"*

Don't allow the enemy to pester your mind with guilt either. You may have failed and people are pointing their fingers at you and what they are saying is true.

- You messed up last week--again! So what?
  Get a *"get back up"* in your mind!
- You flunked yesterday! Big deal! You are not the first person to fail, and you certainly won't be the last one.
  Get a *"get back up"* in your mind!

If you totally blew it, don't stay down—get right back up, brush yourself off and get back in the race. As **Romans 6:1-2** implies, flunking and getting back up is not a license to sin, but it isn't over till Jesus says it's over. Even if it seems that all your strength is gone, keep striving to enter in at the strait *(pearly)* gate and – you – will – make – it!

> *"...and let us run with patience the race that is set before us, Looking unto Jesus the author and finisher of our faith; who for the joy that was set before Him endured the cross, despising the shame, and is set down at the right hand of the throne of God."*

– Hebrews 12:1-2

How To...

Jesus demonstrated that temptation will come our way, but that it is not an insurmountable foe. Every time you resist temptation, it will become easier to resist it the next time it comes around. When you don't resist it, it will be more difficult the next time. You may indeed be lonely on cold winter nights, but you must resist temptation to illicit sexual relations. Common law marriage may be sanctioned by your state, but you must make a clean break from sleeping with your fiancé if you've accepted Christ as your Lord and Savior.

*Make an effort to resist
what the devil throws your way!*

The devil tempted the Lord Jesus in three different areas. He will also switch temptations when he sees that you are resisting

him in one area. Consistently make an effort to resist whatever he throws your way. If you fail even in your thoughts, repent quickly. Talk back to the devil and command him to stop barraging your mind with sinful thoughts. Speak to yourself also and tell your mind not to receive them. This will close the doorway. Repeat this as often as you need to, remembering that Holy Spirit is always here to help you.

- Prioritize your spiritual wellbeing.
- Repel things that have even a tendency to detour you.
- Control your thoughts and run from sexual immorality.
- Resolve that you are going to reach the *Gates of Pearls* with or without your church friends.
- If you fail one temptation, get back up, repent and be on the alert for that temptation the next time it comes around.

"Watch and pray that ye enter not into temptation: the spirit indeed is willing, but the flesh is weak."

– Matthew 26:41

Don't ever give up. Don't be ashamed to seek professional help as well. Keep praying! Every time you have a breakthrough in prayer, remember that you are still a weak human being and your dependency is on Christ. Remember He said, *'Without me you can do nothing."* So say, *"Lord, I thank you for the break-through in prayer. Thank you for the open heaven, but when I leave this mountain top experience, lead me not into temptation. Speak to me when you see me walking into temptation."* Your word says:

"The steps of a good man are ordered by the Lord: and he delighteth in his way."

– Psalms 37:23

"So direct my steps that I may not fall into temptation. I give you permission to intervene on my behalf and deliver me in the Valley of Temptation."

MY PERSONAL THOUGHTS & INSPIRATIONS

CHAPTER 13
Prayer & Faith Lanes

Christians are not exempt from life's trials. We encounter the same struggles that non-believers experience. We drive on the same traffic jammed highways during rush hour, work on the same stressful jobs and have the same demanding schedules. Often, we struggle on our own to resolve the various perplexities of this twenty-first century. Prayer, however, makes a difference. Prayer in these trouble times is critical if we are to run a successful race.

Faith is another powerful resource that should accompany prayer. Prayer and faith are two powerful tools available to us. They are not only tools; they are arsenals – important arsenals to defeat our enemy. By the time you finish this chapter, I hope that you will walk in the power that God slated for you as you journey to the *Gates of Pearls*. I hope also that you'll engage prayer and faith with great intensity and see greater results as you apply these two powerful arsenals.

Prayer and ***faith*** are power twins. Working together, they reach beyond human ability – way out into the Spirit realm and accomplish insurmountable tasks. Prayer and faith form two complimentary lanes on the highway to heaven. Stay in these two lanes and you'll make it home right on time.

Prayer

"The earnest prayer of a righteous man has great power and wonderful results. Elijah was as completely human as we are, and yet when he prayed earnestly that no rain would fall, none fell for the next three and a half years! Then he prayed again, this time that it would rain, and down it poured, and the grass turned green and the gardens began to grow again."

– James 5:16-18 *(TLB)*

From this illustration of the position of prayer, we can deduce that some prayers are fervent and effective while some are not. Prayer that emanates from an honest, sincere, humble heart gets God's attention and produces results. David saw results in his prayer because he was honest and open with God – **Psalms 139**. Even when David sinned, God responded to his prayer of repentance. David understood God's heart. He knew how to get a prayer through.

Prayer is agreeing with God concerning His will here on earth. *Prayer* is the expression of the very nature of our hearts to God. *Prayer* can be spontaneous, but it should not be rigid or ritualistic. Whether in formal, public or private settings, prayer is simply talking with God. Talk with God everywhere!

- **Talk with Him** in the morning.
- **Talk with Him** while driving to work.
- **Talk with Him** when you go to the restroom.
- **Talk with Him** on your way to church.

Jesus said:

"...*men ought always to pray, and not to faint.*"

— **Luke 18:1**

You do not necessarily have to follow a defined format in prayer; you only need to be honest and open when you talk to God, just as you would with a close friend. I concur with the Bible that God moves in a mysterious way and that His ways are past finding out. His response to our prayers may not always be readily recognized, or it may not be realized in the timeframe or in the way we want, but make no mistake about it—God responds to our prayers. God is a covenant God and He always does His part.

"If My people who are called by My name will humble themselves, and pray and seek My face, and turn from their wicked ways, then I will hear from heaven, and will forgive their sin and heal their land. Now My eyes will be open and My ears attentive to prayer made in this place."

— **2 Chronicles 7:14-15** *(NKJV)* emphasis is mine

This confirms that prayer changes things. It shows that God prioritizes our prayers and registers them as reasons for violating adversity around us. It also shows that we must exhibit humility and perseverance along with prayer. It implies that when devastation surrounds us and answers aren't arriving, we should take inventory of our lives to see if there is any sin that's preventing our answers from reaching us. I'm sure we would agree that Christians are praying today about various issues, yet many are not seeing the answers they need. This scripture makes good for preaching, but some Christians cringe to quote it because they have not seen it manifested in their lives. When we don't see God hearing from heaven, forgiving sin and healing the land, we must humble ourselves, check our lives for sin and turn away from it.

> *"Behold, the LORD's hand is not shortened, that it cannot save; neither His ear heavy, that it cannot hear."*

– Isaiah 59:1

Are you seeing answers to your prayers? God's answers are: yes, no or wait. Sometimes the wait is extended, but you should be realizing answers to various other prayers. **James 5:17** shows that we do not have to be the super Christians we think we should be to see results when we pray. Ordinary Christians can expect answers to prayer. Don't just pray to impress God. Don't pray to impress others either, but pray with a purpose. Be specific in your request. Be serious, honest and open with God and you will see results in your prayers.

Prayer is the power supply for success. A life of prayer is a visible characteristic of every Christian who rose to prominence in the history of the Church. Many churches started as prayer groups, who had no intentions of starting a Church. People just followed the strong desire to pray.

Draw God's presence into your home through prayer and you will see positive changes there. Change the attitude of prayer in your church to an atmosphere of inviting God's presence there as well and miracles will begin to happen. When you pray for the sick healing and deliverance will happen. Start a prayer group. Encourage Christians to pray and change the course of our country.

Anti-Christian laws will be reversed as we invoke God's presence through prayer.

Kneeling Power

I cannot put it any other way. If you want to make it to the *Gates of Pearls*, stay in Prayer Lane. Stay on your knees. There can never be too much kneeling. There can never be too much prayer. Before His arrest, trial and crucifixion, Jesus spent long hours in prayer. He prayed until His sweat became like great drops of blood. Sometimes we must pray fervently as well, if we're to see a breakthrough in some circumstances we encounter. The fervent prayer that James talked about is a weapon that defeats demons and tears down Satan's strongholds. Demolishing strongholds is critical if we are to experience answers to prayer. That's why we must be persistent and earnest in prayer. Often, angels are given answers to our prayers, but they are delayed or interrupted by enemy spirits in the heavenly realm.

In the book of **Daniel**, we see *Daniel* praying earnestly. Twenty-one days after he began to pray, an angel showed up. The angel informed Daniel that from the very first day he prayed, God heard and had responded, but the prince of the Kingdom of Persia *(Satan's assigned demon to Persia)* had delayed him. Daniel's persistence in prayer produced the victory. Persistent, earnest prayer is like a continuous onslaught of ballistic missiles released on demonic strongholds. Intense prayer releases God's power, scatters the forces of darkness, and produces positive results. Persistent prayer does not insinuate that God needs to be provoked or that we should go before Him begging every day. On the contrary, persistent

prayer sets the stage for a victorious outcome and refuses to settle for anything less than victory.

Prayer is also more than just making our petitions known or requesting things from God. Prayer is also an exercise in worship. Prayer tells our Father that we honor and reverence Him as God above all other Gods. Prayer has even more significance and importance in heaven's perspective than we think sometimes. Even when we don't receive answers, our prayers still fulfill their greater purpose. Our prayers ascend to God's throne as a sweet aroma that saturates heaven's entire atmosphere. We should remember this often and pray, if only to fill heaven with a most pleasant perfume.

"And when he had taken the book, the four beasts and four and twenty elders fell down before the Lamb, having every one of them harps, **and golden vials full of odours, which are the prayers of saints***."*

– **Revelation 5:8** emphasis is mine.

"And another angel came and stood at the altar, having a golden censer; and there was given unto him much incense, **that he should offer it with the prayers of all saints upon the golden altar** *which was before the throne."*

"And the smoke of the incense, which came with the prayers of the saints, ascended up before God out of the angel's hand."

– **Revelation 8:3-4** emphasis is mine

Pray Until the Heavens Open

> *"For our battle is not against flesh and blood, but against the rulers, against the authorities, against the world powers of this darkness, **against the spiritual forces of evil in the heavens**."*
>
> – **Ephesians 6:12** *(HCSB)* emphasis is mine

I reiterate; we are in a spiritual war!!!

We are fighting against principalities and powers that rule the heavens above us. As seen in Daniel's experience demons are assigned over various territories. They control much of the subsequent actions of the people who live in their territory. They control sickness, disease and even the laws that are enacted in their area. As Christians unite in prayer, these forces are dethroned and significant changes occur. Often, these changes are realized only after extended and persistent periods of united prayer. Some countries are seeing neighborhoods change as Christians disregard denominational differences and unite in prayer. Prayer is our weapon for offence and defense.

Prayer gives us direct access to the third heaven

Paul was caught up in the third heavens. If there is a third heaven, there must be a first and a second heaven. Paul saw demons creating darkness in the heavens *(first or second)* and ruling the darkness there. Persistent prayer burns a hole in this demonic atmosphere of darkness and gives us direct access to the third heaven. This hole in the darkness that prayer creates also gives angels easier access to ascend and descend with answers to our prayers.

"Now it came to pass in the thirtieth year, in the fourth month, in the fifth day of the month, as I was among the captives by the river of Chebar, that the heavens were opened, and I saw visions of God."

– Ezekiel 1:1

Why is it that people came from all over the world to Azusa Street and experienced the outpouring of *Holy Spirit*? God is omnipresent, so He was in their home town just as well. Why couldn't they experience the same outpouring in their own home town or country? Some people fell under the power of the *Holy Spirit* as soon as they got off the train to Azusa Street. Even some of the station workers were slain in the spirit and were heard speaking in tongues.

Why did this mighty outpouring of God's power happen in this vicinity? Because there was an open heaven – a hole in the heavens over Azusa Street. Prayer, fasting, studying God's word and seeking His face in reference to the *Holy Ghost* outpouring, created this hole. The heavens were not open over other areas that didn't persevere in prayer, so they could not experience the power that results from such conditions. God is always everywhere, but we have to break open the heavens through prayer, fasting, studying God's word and seeking His face if we are to experience the same spiritual results.

"Pray in the Spirit at all times and on every occasion. Stay alert and be persistent in your prayers for all believers everywhere."

– Ephesians 6:18 *(NLT)*

Prayer is intensive, spiritual warfare.

Satan knows that the more we pray the weaker he becomes, so he will try anything to keep us from praying. This is the reason why our mind tends to wander during prayer. As we shared earlier, he interjects all kinds of thoughts into our minds to distract us from prayer. Remember **2 Corinthians 10:5** instructs us to *cast down imaginations and bring into captivity every thought to the obedience of Christ?* Vocalizing our prayer helps us to stay focused. Don't stop praying when you feel you have exhausted your vocabulary. This is a very critical junction – the place where success is decided. When we have prayed out, then it's time for us to pray through! Allow *Holy Spirit* to take our intercession into the throne room. Praying in tongues enhances this and is a powerful tool against our enemy.

"For if I pray in an unknown tongue, my spirit prayeth, but my understanding is unfruitful."

– 1 Corinthians 14:14

God is calling us back to prayer. We are going to see strong-holds tumble as we come together and pray. This is the hour of prayer! If your Church does not have regular intercessory prayer, start it right away! Change your neighborhood through prayer.

Faith

We have expounded the subject of prayer, but it is simply not enough just to pray. It is important that we believe God, not only after we see results, but when we pray.

Christians are to walk by faith, not by sight. Faith is, believing what God promised in *His Word* and applying the principles of that belief, instead of acquiescing to the historically bad outcome. Many have wavered at this junction, but close your eyes to the abandoned vehicles you see around you and believe God.

> *"Faith is the confident assurance that something we want to happen is going to happen. It is the certainty that what we hope for is waiting for us, even though we cannot see it up ahead."*

> **– Hebrews 11:1** *(TLB)*

It is essential that we understand that faith works only where God's word is present. **Hebrews 11:3** *(NKJV)* says:

> *"By faith we understand that the worlds were framed by the word of God, so that the things which are seen were not made of things which are visible."*

The *Word of God* is the foundation of faith. We exercise faith by standing on the Word of God. In other words, don't just say that you are believing God for healing. State the healing scripture you are using to support your statement.

*There is no such thing as **Impossible**...*

On earth, we relate to the physical. We relate to things we can see, hear, smell, taste, or touch, but God operates in a realm far beyond our abilities. We operate in the natural, but God operates in the supernatural. With God, there is no such thing as impossible. In creation, God spoke and the non-existent became existent. THAT'S FAITH! Faith originated with God. Faith is His mode of operation. When we use faith then, we touch God. Faith moves God. God responds when He sees faith because faith is His language. **Hebrews 10:38** says: *"The just shall live by faith."*

When Jesus was here He was all God, yet He was all man. Although He was God, Jesus functioned as a man. He depended on God; He believed God and operated in faith. He performed many miracles, but never took credit for any of them. Often, He gave the credit to the individual that experienced the miracle. He told Bartimaeus and the woman who touched His garment: *"Thy faith hath made thee whole."* We need to exercise our faith as well, even if we have only a little. Jesus said as little as a mustard seed of faith can move mountains and He meant it!

You don't need faith where possibility or human ability exists. If you don't have any problems, you don't need faith. We all have problems, but every runner that has ever run this race successfully had to utilize faith. They all had to stay in Faith Lane. This journey is a race in faith. We will face impossible situations; we will encounter challenges for which we don't have the solution, that's when we need faith, that's when we grab faith—and that's when we apply faith.

Miracles by Faith

Opportunities for using faith will arise as long as you stay on Faith Lane. Faith is always the supernatural solution for a problem. As we stare retrospectively at all the miracles in the Bible, we see that the preamble for faith was adversity, difficulty, or some impossible situation. So when we face various challenges, they are just opportunities for us to use faith. How we respond to these challenges matters to God. We should not cringe or give up when we face them. God expects us to stay in Faith Lane and exercise faith.

"Jesus answered and said to them, Have faith in God."
— **Mark 11:22** *(NKJV)*

"If ye have faith as a grain of mustard seed, ye shall say unto this mountain, remove hence to yonder place; and it shall remove; and nothing shall be impossible unto you."

– Matthew 17:20

This was the scripture that God spoke to me early in the 1990s as I sought Him regarding seeing miracles. Before this I had even preached about faith, but applying faith was a different story. Ever since then I have exercised faith in various difficult situations and have experienced significant miracles. I am assured now that faith accomplishes more than human ability. When we mix faith with prayer we break through the Spirit realm, pull down our enemy's strongholds, and experience what God intends for us.

Rain Miracle:

Back in the 1990s, I did an outdoor revival in *Barbados*. We did not have a tent; all we had was a wooden stage that we set up in a parking lot. Rain was forecasted every day, but I prayed against it and exercise faith. The rain held until about the fourth night. As I began to read the scripture, the rain began, so someone handed me an umbrella and I held it over my Bible. When I finished reading the scripture the rain was still falling, but I put away the umbrella and believed God to stop the rain. The rain stopped almost immediately.

The next night someone who lived within walking distance of the parking lot said that as they walked home from the meeting the previous night, the streets were so flooded with water, they thought a water main had been broken. The rain poured just walking distance away, but not in the parking lot where we were. Prayer mixed with faith brought great results!

Renovation Miracle:

When I started pastoring Mount Carmel in 1997, it was behind in the mortgage and the members were struggling just to keep the lights on. The title of my first sermon was *"The sky will be the limit."* I said that God had been blessing me over the years and I believed that as long as I was pastoring there, Mount Carmel would be a recipient of some of the blessings that God had been sending my way. <u>One month later</u>, a pastor gave me a check for **sixty-seven hundred dollars** to pay off the mortgage. He said *God told him to give me the money.*

The building needed much repairs so we launched a renovation project. A lady heard about this and gave seventy-five thousand dollars towards the roof. Well, our adversary was not very happy about what God had done, so he came against us with vicious contempt. In 2002, we lost over half our membership, but we walked in faith and took a new mortgage for over three hundred thousand dollars to renovate the building.

When the renovation was completed, the contractor gave us a bill for $45,000. We had spent all the money and had started repaying the mortgage. The contractor asked if we could pay $1,000. per month. I said, *"No, we can't."* He asked, *"How about $500. per month?"* I said, *"No, we can't do that either, but I'll talk with you later."* He said he owed the electrical contractor $13,000. and that if we could come up with that amount, we could negotiate a monthly payment for the balance. I said, *"I'll talk with you later"* and laugh all along. I said to myself, *"We don't have any money left, so what should I do; Cry?"* NO! I held my head back and laughed.

On my way to work I talked with God. I said, *"God, the contractor was very nice to me, so I don't want to insult him. I don't want to tell him that we don't have the money. We have been*

paying him all along, so he doesn't know that we don't have anymore money. I need $13,000. I don't know who has it but You do." The same night a member called to say that ***she would give us $13,000***.

We struggled to pay the balance and a few more miracles took place to help us, until the last $15,000. We were desperate again. I asked the Lord again and reminded the congregation that God had given us the first amount and requested that they join me in asking Him for the remainder. The next Sunday someone *(not a member)* gave us a check for $15,000. Bless God! Faith works!

Beyond Miracles

"But Pastor Eversel, when am I going to see my miracle?" These are examples of miracles that came through faith, but faith is far greater, much deeper and wider than miracles. Faith endures even when a miraculous outcome is not realized. After listing the successes of the great patriots, **Hebrews 11**, the faith chapter added:

> *"Others were tortured, not accepting deliverance, that they might obtain a better resurrection. Still others had trial of mockings and scourgings, yes, and of chains and imprisonment. They were stoned, they were sawn in two, were tempted, were slain with the sword...*
>
> *....And all these, having obtained a good testimony through faith, did not receive the promise, God having provided something better for us, that they should not be made perfect apart from us."*
>
> **– Hebrews 11:35-40**

This shows that faith does not necessarily exempt one from adversity or prolong hardship, or that tragedy does not necessarily mean that we have less faith. Actually, it takes more faith to continue when there is no end in sight, than when we experience a miraculous deliverance.

No one on this road escapes challenges or obstacles, but faith forms an obstacle to obstacles. Faith deflates obstacles. In **Matthew 21:21** –

> *"Jesus answered and said unto them, Verily I say unto you, If ye have faith, and doubt not, ye shall not only do this which is done to the fig tree, but also if ye shall say unto this mountain, Be thou removed, and be thou cast into the sea; it shall be done."*

You may be saying, *"This scripture is easy to quote but, how long will it be before the mountain moves? How much more do I have to endure before I see a change?"* If the mountain never moves, will you lose faith? Whether or not the mountain moves, the end of faith is success, not necessarily a miracle. Success is the only thing at the end of faith. If you have not realized success, it only means that you are not yet at the end of faith.

- ***Failure*** is not in the Christians vocabulary – faith is!
- You'll only know *failure* if you *believe it* and *accept it*.
- ***Perseverance*** is the opposite of *failure*.
- ***Perseverance*** is *getting back up every time you fall* – Getting back up and getting back up until you succeed.

> *"Brothers and sisters, I do not consider myself yet to have taken hold of it. But one thing I do:*

Forgetting what is behind and straining toward what is ahead."

– Philippians 3:13 *(NIV)*

After you have prayed, stand on the promises of God's word. Don't move! Dig your heels in like a stubborn mule and resolve that you will experience the things you have prayed for. Applying faith dictates that you stand on the *Word of God* instead of buckling under pressure. When you mix prayer and faith, the impossible becomes possible. This is what Jesus meant when He said that nothing would be impossible to us. Prayer and faith is a combination that shuts up the devil, makes him take his tent down, pack up his stuff and go home with his tail between his legs. **Mark 11:24** *(NKJV)* sums it up this way:

*"Therefore I say to you, whatever things you ask **when you pray, believe that you receive them, and you will have them**."*

emphasis is mine

It is important to believe God before you see results. There are mountains up ahead, but Faith Lane runs right through them. Especially today, you must engage faith to reach the other side. Jesus told Thomas:

"Because you have seen Me, have you believed? Blessed are they who did not see, and yet believed."

– John 20:29 *(NASB)*

So, take **Mark 11:24** literally. You will realize answers to your prayers even if you can muster only a mustard seed of faith to believe that you receive before you see.

How To...

To survive the perils of the twenty-first century and make it to the holy city, stay in Prayer and Faith Lanes. Those who made it through the gates spent time in prayer and held on in faith. Set aside a daily time to pray. For most people, early in the morning is best. Set your alarm. You may fail often, but always ask *Holy Spirit* to help you again to meet your appointment. Remember, *"Effort, not perfection."* We cannot lay our armor down; not even a second before the finish line. We must persevere day after day until we reach the *Gates of Pearls*.

- Stay on your knees before the Lord Jesus and ask Him to give you the strength to survive each challenge.

- Start a prayer group. Encourage Christians to pray and see the course of our country change.

- Pray, if only to send up material that creates a sweet aroma all over heaven.

- Study God's word and allow it to abide in you – **John 15:7**.

- Don't ever get tired waiting on God – **Isaiah 40:31**.

- Remember, success is the only thing waiting for you at the end of faith. Stay on the road until success greets you, even if this is after you pass through the *Gates of Pearls*.

- Remember daily also, that God responds to faith. Here is a simple way to apply faith principles. Just remember this acronym *(CAT)*. Apply the following suggestions daily and it will change your life. The principles may not corroborate your traditional or religious beliefs, but they originate from God's word. Note that they all deal with what you SAY – **Mark 11:23** –

C – Command the devil to take his hands off your possessions, especially your finances!

"Behold, I give unto you power to tread on serpents and scorpions, and over all the power of the enemy: and nothing shall by any means hurt you."

– **Luke 10:19**

A – Ask ministering spirits *(angels)* to gather the resources you need!

"Are they not all ministering spirits, sent forth to minister for them who shall be heirs of salvation?"

– **Hebrews 1:14**

T – Thank God for supplying your need even before you see it!

"Father, thank you for hearing me. (You always hear me, of course, but I said it because of all these people standing here, so that they will believe you sent me.) Then He shouted, "Lazarus, come out!"

– **John 11:41-43** *(TLB)*

CHAPTER 14
TO THE
GATES OF PEARLS

There is much secular humor regarding Peter at the *Gates of Pearls* and who he does or does not allow to enter. But there is no quiz at the gate and Peter is not there; angels are there. They are there to allow only those with valid passports to enter. Christians reach the *Gates of Pearls* either through the glorious gathering of the saints *(rapture)* or, early transition *(death)*. I cannot complete this or any other book without talking about the rapture. This event is too imminent and too important. We don't think of the rapture as we should, but Jesus said it would happen this way.

"Therefore be ye also ready: for in such an hour as ye think not the Son of Man cometh."

– Matthew 24:44

The world however, is getting suspicious. People are sensing that something catastrophic is about to happen. Recently, there has been much conjecture in the media and in general conversations regarding the end of the world. Prophecies, the Mayan calendar, Nostradamus, all allude to the soon end of man's existence. There have even been predictions of a specific day when the world will end. From our position in the prophetic list of events however, more catastrophic events are soon to be unleashed in Planet Earth, and the Lord Jesus will return soon. In **Matthew 24**, Jesus spoke about the signs of His return: Famines, economic difficulties, natural disasters, diseases, wars and other devastations will precede His second coming.

> *"Therefore keep watch, because you do not know on what day your Lord will come. But understand this: If the owner of the house had known at what time of night the thief was coming, he would have kept watch and would not have let his house be broken into. So you also must be ready, because the Son of Man will come at an hour when you do not expect him."*
>
> **– Matthew 24:42-43** *(NIV)*

The Book of **Revelation** speaks explicitly about the end of the world, but it does not speak much about the rapture. The rapture however, is the central doctrine of Christianity. The word rapture is derived from the Greek word ***parousia*** meaning *appearing or arrival*. This event speaks of the sudden, secret appearing of our Lord and Savior Jesus in the clouds, and the immediate taking away of all His true followers. We will be escorted to the Judgment seat of Christ and rewarded for our Christian service.

> *"And, behold, I come quickly; and my reward is with me, to give every man according as his work shall be."*
>
> **– Revelation 22:12**

This return of Christ is mentioned over three hundred times in the *New Testament*. Paul writes about it numerous times. **Mathew 24** and **Mark 13** address the subject extensively as well as first and second Thessalonians.

> *"For the Lord Himself will descend from heaven with a shout, with the voice of the archangel and with the trumpet of God, and the dead in Christ will rise first. Then we who are alive and remain will be caught up together with them in the clouds to meet the Lord in the air, and so we shall always be with the Lord. Therefore, comfort one another with these words."*
>
> **– 1 Thessalonians 4:16-18** *(NASU)*

There are different schools of thought regarding the time of the rapture. Most evangelical Bible scholars believe that all prophetic scriptures relative to events that will precede the rapture have already taken place. They believe that our present Church Age is awaiting the first stage of the second coming of Christ. Contrary to many recent last-day experts however, no one knows the exact day of Christ's second coming. Jesus advised us to be ready when He returns. If you have the time, the energy and the biblical education to debate the different schools of thoughts regarding the time of the rapture, then go ahead and debate. My council however, would be that you should not spend much time worrying about such matters. More important than knowledge of any of the theological positions on the time of the rapture, is that you are ready when it happens.

The rapture will take place...

> *"In a moment, in a twinkling of an eye."*
>
> **– 1 Corinthians 15:52**

Some Christians will be unprepared and will miss it. For those raptured, however, it will be grandeur instead of gloom, the sudden end of all worries and cares, and the exhilaration of seeing the Lord Jesus Christ face to face.

> *"Then shall two be in the field; the one shall be taken, and the other left."*

> **– Matthew 24:40**

In **John 11:25** Jesus said:

> *"I am the resurrection, and the life: he that believeth in Me, though he were dead, yet shall he live."*

We should all know it, yet I must say: *"Saints don't die, they just slip away."* Jesus gives eternal life which begins the moment we accept Him as Lord and Savior. Death for the saints is therefore, an early transition to glory.

Early Transition

Psalms 116:15 says:

> *"Precious in the sight of the Lord is the death of His saints."*

Most of us do not think of death this way. We do not look at it as a means of entrance through the Gates of Pearls, but many of our loved ones have passed through the gates that way.

> *"And now, dear brothers and sisters, we want you to know what will happen to the believers who*

have died so you will not grieve like people who have no hope."

– 1 Thessalonians 4:13 (NLT)

Many of us will cross that river of death one day, but the Bible clearly teaches that death is simply the separation of our body, soul, and spirit and that it is certainly not the end of our existence.

In **Genesis** God said:

"Let us make man in our own image."

God is a triune being. That is, **God** as *Father*, *Son* and *Holy Spirit*. Since man was made in God's image, man is also a *tripartite* being, made up of *body, soul and spirit*. As long as these three are united life is experienced. When they separate, natural death is realized since the body cannot exist on its own. Natural death is therefore the separation of the body, soul and spirit of man. The spirit returns to God (**Eccl 12:7**) and the soul goes to heaven or hell depending on the person's decision for Christ while they lived. (**Matt 10:28**, **Acts 2:31** & **Rev 20:4**)

Soon after I started pastoring, a member called me to discuss the things she wanted done when she expired. I was astounded at how candid she was about her death. She wasn't ill; she was far from dying. She had however, settled everything about life and was ready to go. Years later, I am now amazed at how candidly I have been able to preach, teach and write about death as well. Normally, death is not pleasant to even think about. The very thought of death brings back significant sorrow and often reopen wounds caused when death snatched some loved one from us at a very sudden and least expected time.

A preacher must face the cold reality of death because we are the ones positioned to take control of the situation and help people through their bereavement. Preachers face the cold reality that other than by the rapture, none of us are getting out alive. In **Genesis 2:17**, God told Adam:

"...in the day that thou eatest thereof thou shalt surely die."

Adam ate of the tree and man has been dying ever since. So, none of us came to stay forever. We come; we create our mark in the sands of time, and then we leave. Leaving here is inevitable. **Ecclesiastes 9:5** says:

"The living know that they shall die."

We did not have a choice of when to be born, where we would be born or to whom we would be born. It's almost the same with dying. The chilling hands of death unexpectedly snatch most people. Although we do not necessarily have a choice of where or when we die, we have a choice of where we go after we die.

Home

To the believer heaven is home. The African American Christian community refers to the funeral service for Christians as the *"Home Going Service."* While close friends and relatives sit in tears, other church members celebrate the home going of the deceased. When I say celebrate, I mean celebrate! Some dance and shout just as they do in regular church settings. We celebrate the hope that death is only a temporary separation.

> *"There are many homes up there where my Father lives and I am going to prepare them for your coming. When everything is ready, then I will come and get you, so that you can always be with me where I am. If this weren't so, I would tell you plainly."*
>
> – **John 14:2-4** *(TLB)*

Whether we die or whether we are raptured will make little difference to us because all born again, blood washed children of God will be home. **Hebrews 13:14** says:

> *"For here have we no continuing city, but we seek one to come."*

City gates made of pearls

This earth is not our home; it is only our temporary place of abode. We are just nomads on this earth. We are on our way to a city whose gates are made of pearls. There at the big, white finish line, Jesus stands arrayed in all His glory. When we get there, those of us who would have experienced death will look back on the event as just the means of an early transition to glory. Whether we get there through death or through the rapture, all of us would have left our earthly houses, just to walk through those gates to glory.

> *"Behold, I tell you a mystery: We shall not all sleep, but we shall all be changed—in a moment, in the twinkling of an eye, at the last trumpet. For the trumpet will sound and the dead will be raised incorruptible, and we shall be changed."*
>
> – **1 Corinthians 15:51-52** *(NKJV)*

Somebody ought to remind that old devil that saints don't die; they just slip away. I can think of some who literally did. On her sick bed, one church mother raised her hands and praised the Lord Jesus Christ, then lowered her hands, closed her eyes and went on to be with Him. A minister from our church: A few hours before she died asked her care giver, *"Can't you hear them singing? They are singing so beautiful."* **2 Corinthians 5:8** says:

"We are confident, I say, and willing rather to be absent from the body, and to be present with the Lord."

There is a finish line and there is a reward at the end.

One of these days, I'm going to pick up my hat,
put on my shoes and get out of here!
Where are you going Brother Pastor?
I am going home – I'm going to the *Gates of Pearls*.
It doesn't matter if my eyes are closed in death.
Don't you think for a moment that I missed it! No!
I just crossed the finished line – I just reached my destination.

"Henceforth there is laid up for me a crown of righteousness, which the Lord, the righteous judge, shall give me at that day: and not to me only, but unto all them also that love his appearing."

– 2 Timothy 4:8

One of these days, I'm going to defy the laws of gravity and rise – and rise – and rise, and go on home to be with Jesus. It will be exciting to see *Peter, Paul, Silas, Wigglesworth,* and other great men and women of God. I hope to meet them all, but bless God; I want to see Jesus first. Paul said in **Philippians 3:10 –**

"That I may know Him, and the power of His resurrection, and the fellowship of His sufferings, being made conformable unto His death."

One of these days, I'm going to be gone – in the twinkling of an eye. One of these days I'm going home – I may not have time to say goodbye, but bless God – bless God – bless God, I'm going home!

Like *Abraham* in **Hebrews 11:10**, I am looking *"for a city which hath foundations, whose builder and maker is God."*

If I die, this corruptible will put on incorruption.
If I'm alive, this mortal will put on immortality.
One way or the other, I'm going to the *Gates of Pearls!*

"So when this corruptible shall have put on incorruption, and this mortal shall have put on immortality, then shall be brought to pass the saying that is written, Death is swallowed up in victory. **O death, where is thy sting? O grave, where is thy victory?** *The sting of death is sin; and the strength of sin is the law. But thanks be to God, which giveth us the victory through our Lord Jesus Christ."*

– **1 Corinthians 15:54-57** emphasis is mine

Ensure you are ready because this plane to glory is about to take off. We're about to take off from *Planet Earth*. Soon Jesus is going to roll back the clouds and call us home. I don't know if it will be today, tomorrow or next week, but any day now we are expecting the trumpet call to go home. Wherever we are on this road to glory angels will snatch us up and immediately transport us to the portals of glory. We are going to see friends who have gone on before us. They are anxiously awaiting our arrival.

How To...

- **The rapture of the Church is imminent.**
  Strive to live daily in readiness for this great event.

- **Remember always:**
  that heaven is our home and we enter it through the ***Gates of Pearls****.*

- **Remember always:**
  Saints don't die, they just slip away.

When trials or difficulties overwhelm you, think of the *Gates of Pearls* as a reason to persevere until you see them. Think of our blessed redeemer. Think of Him all the day long. Think of that day when we pass through the gates of the city and behold our Savior: *The Lamb of God* – **The Lord Jesus Christ.**

CHAPTER 15

THE VICTORIOUS BRIDE

*"He then carried me away in the Spirit to a great and high mountain and showed me the holy city, Jerusalem, coming down out of heaven from God, arrayed with God's glory. Her radiance was like a very precious stone, like a jasper stone, bright as crystal. The city had a massive high wall, with 12 gates. Twelve angels were at the gates;…. There were three gates on the east, three gates on the north, three gates on the south, and three gates on the west…The **12 gates are 12 pearls; each individual gate was made of a single pearl**. The broad street of the city was pure gold, like transparent glass. I did not see a sanctuary in it, because the Lord God the Almighty and the Lamb are its sanctuary. The city does not need the sun or the moon to shine on it, because God's glory illuminates it, **and its lamp is the Lamb**."*

– Revelation 21:10-13 & 21-23 *(HCSB)*
emphasis is mine

W e have talked about various challenges along the way to the Gates of Pearls. We have also discussed the requirements for getting on the road and for staying on the road. We have looked at the assistance heaven provides us as we journey, but reaching the Gates of Pearls is not the end; it is only the beginning. Passing through the Gates of Pearls, meeting the Lord our Savior Jesus Christ, experiencing the majesty of the place He has prepared for us and receiving our reward is our ultimate goal. It has to be that the splendor of this city surpasses all our imagination. Those songwriters I mentioned in chapter one, left us their previews of the majesty of this city beyond the gates. One said that it was *"Springtime Forever."* Some talked about having a new body. Others talked about rest for the weary, while others shared their desire to be "Living where the healing waters flow." They also talked about the marriage supper of the Lamb and the white robes of the bride of Christ. We are the bride of Christ.

The Bride of Christ

With great anticipation, the bride of Christ should look forward to the great ***Marriage Supper of the Lamb***. The Lamb's wife holds a position of unmatched splendor. The *Lamb's wife* must therefore possess peculiar, yet specific qualities, since we will be presented to Jesus Christ as a perfect bride. **Ephesians 5:25-27** lists some of the pertinent characteristics of the bride:

> *"Husbands, love your wives, just as Christ loved the church and gave Himself up for her to make her holy, **cleansing her** by the washing with water*

*through the word, and to **present her** to Himself as a radiant church, **without stain or wrinkle or any other blemish, but holy and blameless**."*

Emphasis is mine

Defining the characteristics I have highlighted shows all of them interwoven and connected by a cord of holiness and purity:

a. **Holy** – *Known for righteous actions* – **Rev 19:7-8**.
b. **Cleansed** and **washed** – *by the Word of God*.
c. **A radiant Church** – *A Church reflecting the light of God*.
d. **Without stain or wrinkle** – *A spotless Church*.
e. **Without blemish** – *A pure virgin* – **2 Cor 11:2**.
f. **Holy & Blameless** – *Meeting the demands of holiness*.

As the *bride of Christ*, we must be aware of the high expectations of the bridegroom. The invitation to be part of the bride of Christ is open to everyone, but don't ever think the Lord has lowered His standards. They are as high as they have always been. It is an honor, a privilege and a blessing beyond human comprehension, not only to be invited to the marriage supper of the Lamb, but to attend.

"Blessed are those who are invited to the wedding feast of the Lamb." And he added, "God Himself has stated this."

– **Revelation 19:9** *(TLB)*

1. The *bride of Christ* must be a ready bride – **Rev 19:7**.
"Let us be glad and rejoice, and give honour to Him: for the marriage of the Lamb is come and His wife hath made herself ready."

2. The bride of Christ must be a righteous bride – **Rev 19:8**.
"And to her was granted that she should be arrayed in fine linen, clean and white: for the fine linen is the righteousness of saints."

3. The bride of Christ must be a fasting bride – **Mark 2:19**.
"And Jesus said unto them, Can the friends of the bridegroom fast, as long as the bridegroom is with them? But the days will come, when the bridegroom shall be taken from them, and then shall they fast."

Fasting helps us to bring our bodies into subjection to God's will and to overcome various temptations in the flesh.

4. The bride of Christ must be a soul winning bride – **Dan 2:3**.
"And they that be wise shall shine as the brightness of the firmament; and they that turn many to righteousness as the stars forever and ever."

If every born again believer would win just one soul for Christ, the entire world would be won for Christ in under five years. Try to win at least one soul for Christ, so you'll receive commendation when you stand before Him.

5. The bride of Christ must be a victorious bride – **Rev 12:11**.
"And they overcame him by the blood of the Lamb and by the word of their testimony; and they loved not their lives unto the death."

This victory must be realized while we are on earth. Those who reach the holy city would have fought against our enemy and defeated him in many battles here on earth, not in heaven.

Jesus never promised us a bed of roses. Even if He did, even a beautiful, tender rose comes not without thorns. Jesus promised that in this world we would have trouble, but He also reiterated that He had already overcome the world, so we could triumph over it as well. The road to the Gates of Pearls is tedious and treacherous and many of those who begin do not continue all the way to the end. As the parable of the sower implies, seventy-five percent find this road too strict and turn back for various reasons. Some fall to temptation and take premature exits, while others are deceived by false advertisement. Twenty-five percent however mature and produce fruit. These are the overcomers. These are those who will stand and receive their rewards. If you were promised an easy road to the Gates of Pearls, wake up! Jesus promised us a cross. Artillery comes at us from all directions and from every angle, but we can overcome. Reaching the gates will be worth it all! Trials of the way will seem as nothing when we get to the finish line. We must overcome!

– Rev 2-17

*"To him that **overcometh** will I give to eat of the hidden manna, and will give him a white stone, and in the stone a new name written, which no man knoweth saving he that receiveth it."*

– Rev 3-5

*"He that **overcometh**, the same shall be clothed in white raiment."*

– Rev 3-12

*"Him that **overcometh** will I make a pillar in the temple of my God, and he shall go no more out: and I will write upon him the name of my God, and the name of the city of my God, which is new Jerusalem,*

*which cometh down out of heaven from my God: and
I will write upon him my new name."*

Emphasis is mine

The Marriage Supper of the Lamb

As the *bride of Christ*, we must be watchful, prayerful and ready to meet our Lord and Savior Jesus Christ. Heaven has been planning this great marriage supper for over two thousand years. It will be a matchless event. Will you be there for this auspicious occasion? Don't miss it for the world. The invitation is so priceless, it is free. In **Matthew 13:46**, Jesus told a story of a merchant:

"Who, when he had found one pearl of great price, went and sold all that he had, and bought it."

The Gates of Pearls are pearls of great price. If you have to give up everything to get there, just get there. Heaven will surely be worth it.

"Then I heard again what sounded like the shouting of a huge crowd, or like the waves of a hundred oceans crashing on the shore, or like the mighty rolling of great thunder, "Praise the Lord. For the Lord our God, the Almighty, reigns. Let us be glad and rejoice and honor Him; for the time has come for the wedding banquet of the Lamb, and His bride has prepared herself."

– Revelation 19:6-7 *(TLB)*

Jesus gave all that He had to make us His bride. He gave up even His throne. Can you comprehend that? Christianity is not about what we can do for God, but what God did for us. Christianity is God seeking man in the person of Jesus Christ. None can truly fathom the love Jesus has for His bride. What love would cause someone who was seated at the right hand of God Almighty, to leave such a position of unspeakable splendor, to come to earth, below the level of man, to die for man, just to give man an opportunity to go to heaven? That's Jesus! But He did more than that. He proposed to us. He offered us His hand in marriage. I could live to be a thousand years; I still could not fathom this love of our *Lord and Savior* **Jesus Christ**.

A Man Called Jesus

Over 700 hundred years before Jesus came, **Isaiah** saw Him:

"Surely He hath borne our griefs and carried our sorrows: yet we did esteem Him stricken, smitten of God, and afflicted. But He was wounded for our transgressions; He was bruised for our iniquities: the chastisement of our peace was upon Him; and with His stripes we are healed."

– Isaiah 53:4-5

While Jesus was still seated at the right hand of majesty, Isaiah prophesied:

"Behold, a virgin shall conceive, and bear a son, and shall call His name Immanuel."

– Isaiah 7:14

When Jesus arrived on the scene, angels left their habitation in heaven and headed for Bethlehem to announce that peace and good will had come to all mankind. When Jesus taught, grace, peace and deliverance flowed from His lips. People...

> *"...were astonished at His doctrine: for He taught them as one that had authority, and not as the scribes."*

> **– Mark 1:22**

Some tried to describe Him, but they were dumbfounded. They could only express that *"a greater than Solomon is here."* Oh! Do you remember when you first met Jesus? Do you remember when He reached down His nail scarred hands and saved you? Oh! Some people get happy just thinking about the goodness of Jesus. Some people say that He is the Rose of Sharon. I really don't know what that means, but I understand when others describe Him as the *Lilly of the valley* and the *Bright and Morning Star*. They also say *He is a Battle Axe*. I must confess that I can only visualize what that means, but I know what they are talking about when they add that *He is a Shelter in the time of storm*. If you know what I'm talking about JUST HOLLER!

When Mary saw Him outside the garden tomb, she thought He was the gardener, but when He said, *"Mary"* she was lost for words to answer Him. She could only say, *"Rabboni; which is to say, Master."* Can you think of words to describe Him? How will you respond when He calls you by your first name? Oh! When I think of the goodness of Jesus and all He's done for me!!!

In **Revelation** chapter one, John saw Him robed in His glorified personality. Although John was one of His close disciples,

John didn't recognize Him because His radiance was brighter than the sun. John could only say He was like the Son of Man, so Jesus identified Himself:

> *"I am Alpha and Omega, the beginning and the ending, saith the Lord, which is, and which was, and which is to come, the Almighty. ...I am He that liveth, and was dead; and, behold, I am alive for evermore, Amen; and have the keys of hell and of death."*
>
> **– Revelation 1:8 & 18**

There is no single description of Jesus' character and personality. No one could truly describe Him, so Jesus described Himself to the seven churches in Asia – **Revelation 2 &3**:

To Ephesus –
> *"....He that holdeth the seven stars in His right hand, who walketh in the midst of the seven golden candlesticks."*

To Smyrna –
> *"...the first and the last, which was dead, and is alive."*

To Pergamos –
> *"...He which hath the sharp sword with two edges."*

To Thyatira –
> *"....the Son of God, who hath His eyes like unto a flame of fire, and His feet are like fine brass."*

To Sardis –

> *"He that hath the seven Spirits of God, and the seven stars."*

To Philadelphia –

> *... He that is holy, He that is true, He that hath the key of David, He that openeth, and no man shutteth; and shutteth, and no man openeth."*

To Laodicea –

> *"...the Amen, the faithful and true witness, the beginning of the creation of God."*

Adoration in Heaven

Although Jesus paid a great price and even died for man's redemption, many people don't care much for Him down here. Some even use His precious, holy name as a swearword, but Jesus is highly exalted in heaven. All throughout heaven, angels worship Him, elders bow down before Him and all the saints adore Him.

> *"He went and took the scroll from the right hand of Him who sat on the throne. And when He had taken it, the four living creatures and the twenty-four elders fell down before the Lamb. ....And they sang a new song, saying:* ***"You are worthy to take the scroll and to open its seals, because you were slain, and with your blood you purchased for God persons from every tribe and language and people and nation.*** *You have made them to be a kingdom*

and priests to serve our God, and they will reign on the earth"

Then I looked and heard the voice of many angels, numbering thousands upon thousands, and ten thousand times ten thousand. They encircled the throne and the living creatures and the elders. In a loud voice they were saying:

"Worthy is the Lamb, who was slain, to receive power and wealth and wisdom and strength and honor and glory and praise!"

Then I heard every creature in heaven and on earth and under the earth and on the sea, and all that is in them, saying:

"To Him who sits on the throne and to the Lamb, be praise and honor and glory and power, forever and ever!" The four living creatures said, "Amen," and the elders fell down and worshiped."

– **Revelation 5:7-14**, emphasis is mine

When They Crown Him
King of Kings and Lord of Lords

Many; Yes! Many Christians are waiting for us beyond the Gates of Pearls. They are excited because they sense that we'll soon be there. They won't start the marriage supper without the raptured Church.

- Will you make it to the *Gates of Pearls*?

- Will you cross the finish line?

- Will you enter through the gates and into the city?

- Will you be at the great marriage supper of the Lamb?

- Will you be there when they crown Jesus *King of Kings* and *Lord of Lords*?

- Will you be there to look into His eyes that are as a flame of fire, yet love personified?

- Will you admire the many crowns on His head?

- Will you ask Him about that name written on Him that no man knows but He himself?

- Will you be there to hear:
  "...the multitude as the voice of many waters and as the voice of mighty thundering, say, Alleluia: for the Lord God omnipotent reigneth?"

– Revelation 19:6

Our eligibility for entrance to heaven cost Jesus a great deal. From the time of His arrest in the garden of Gethsemane to Calvary, Jesus suffered ridicule, was spat on and His friends forsook Him. He was beaten and chunks of flesh came out of His back with every stroke of the Roman whip. They nailed His hands and His feet to the cross and raised it between two thieves. His blood spilled there at Calvary until He died. Satan thought he had won a great victory, but Jesus' death was not the end. Jesus went to hell and took the keys of death and hell. Jesus did all this, just for us. Because of His great sacrifice for lost man, Jesus is highly exalted in heaven. All over heaven, angels bow in worship just at the mention of His name.

Over the centuries, many have found solace at Jesus' feet. Many have found forgiveness for sins there as well. From His eternally

outstretched arms, many have experienced His love and compassion and millions have found peace for their restless souls. Since Calvary *(and only through Calvary)*, millions have reached the *Gates of Pearls.* Oh yes! Many have gone to that place called heaven all because of what Jesus did on the cross. I can think of many that I believe have already made it there. One of these days, the saints from all ages will assemble in heaven as Jesus is crowned:

King of Kings and Lord of Lords!
Will you be there for this grand event?

Moses – will be there with his face shining; *reflecting the glory of God.*

Abraham – the father of faith will be there along with Sarah, Isaac and Jacob.

David – the man after God's own heart will be there as well, maybe as the choir director.

Joshua & Caleb – will be there as well.

All the saints will be dressed in spotless white linen robes. As God's light shines on us, our white robes will reflect glistening white light that will extend all across heaven, since darkness won't have a place there.

Will you be there for this great event?

Award Ceremony

- The saints will receive various awards and recognitions.
- Martyrs for the gospel will receive their martyr's crowns.
- Those who were faithful through temptations and tribulations will receive a crown of life – **James 1:12** & **Rev 2:10.**
- Those who love His appearing will receive a crown of righteousness – **2 Tim 4:8**.
- Many will receive a crown of glory that fadeth not away
  – **1 Peter 5:4**.

  – Will you be there for this majestic event?
  – What kind of crown will you receive?
  – Will there be any stars in your crown?

  "Behold, I come quickly: hold that fast which thou hast, that no man take thy crown."

  ### – Revelation 3:11

I envision a timeless procession of all the saints of the ages, stepping forward to receive their crowns, pearls, stones and stars placed in prominent positions in their crowns. All their earthly labors, sacrifices and trials they overcame will be announced. As the Lord Jesus Himself hands them their well deserved awards, all the saints will applaud loud and long in inexpressible jubilation.

Will you be there for this magnificent event?

This award ceremony will seem like it will go on forever, but that's only until we become acclimated with eternity. The Lord Jesus will take time to detail the recognition of all the saints; even those who made it in by the skin of their teeth. All those whose works withstand the fire will receive a great reward (**1 Cor 3:13**). Then, when the last saint receives his/her reward, there will be another applaud that will seem to last for eternity. I can almost envision the sound of it; getting louder and louder and louder in anticipation of the grandest and most anticipated announcement since the beginning of time and throughout all eternity: Time *(eternity)* for Jesus to be crowned *King of Kings* and *Lord of Lords*. Will you be there for this glorious event?

> *"And I saw heaven opened, and behold a white horse; and He that sat upon Him was called Faithful and True, and in righteousness He doth judge and make war.*
>
> *His eyes were as a flame of fire, and on His head were many crowns; and He had a name written, that no man knew, but He himself.*
>
> *And He was clothed with a vesture dipped in blood: and His name is called The Word of God. And the armies which were in heaven followed Him upon white horses, clothed in fine linen, white and clean...*
>
> *"...And He hath on His vesture and on His thigh a name written, KING OF KINGS, AND LORD OF LORDS."*

– Revelation 19:11-16

Will you be there for this majestic event – when they crown **Jesus** *Kings of Kings* and *Lord of Lords*? It will cost you something to make it there, but not a dime more than what you have. If you surrender to Jesus today and remain surrendered to Him until the day He calls you home, you will be there when they crown Him KING OF KINGS AND LORD OF LORDS.

How To...

"But thou, O man of God, flee these things; and follow after righteousness, godliness, faith, love, patience, meekness. Fight the good fight of faith, lay hold on eternal life, where-unto thou art also called, and hast professed a good profession before many witnesses. I give thee charge in the sight of God, who quickeneth all things, and before Christ Jesus, who before Pontius Pilate witnessed a good confession; That thou keep this commandment without spot, unrebukable, until the appearing of our Lord Jesus Christ: Which in His times He shall shew, who is the blessed and only Potentate, the King of Kings, and Lord of Lord."

– **1 Timothy 6:11-15**, emphasis is mine

Be There!

With patient resolve, look forward to laying your armor down – your helmet, your sword, your shield, your belt and your shoes. You won't need them after you past the *Gates of Pearls*.

- Look forward to wearing a golden, starry, shining crown which has your name boldly inscribed in it.

- Look forward to walking on the streets that are paved with gold.

- Look forward to strolling by the river of life.

- Look forward to seeing Jesus!

We can only imagine the majesty of life beyond the Gates of Pearls.

"That is what is meant by the Scriptures which say that no mere man has ever seen, heard, or even imagined what wonderful things God has ready for those who love the Lord."

– **1 Corinthians 2:9** *(TLB)*

God bless you!

See you at the gates – the **Gates of Pearls**!
  Oh! *Lamb of God we humbly bow in Your presence.*

MY PERSONAL THOUGHTS & INSPIRATIONS

Preparation For Eternity

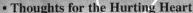

Jesus is coming back for His church...

- **Thoughts for the Hurting Heart**
- **Thoughts from HIS Heart**
  An Urgent Message For Twenty-First Century Christians
- **Thoughts for the 21st Century Pastor**
  A pastor's Resource Guide
- **The Lake of Fire**
- **Through Gates of Pearls** *A Personal Roadmap To Glory*

...Question is-
Are you ready to meet Him?

EMG Publications Book Order Form

BOOK TITLE:	QUANTITY	COST PER BOOK	SHIPPING & HANDLING PER BOOK	SUB TOTAL	TOTAL ENCLOSED
Thoughts For The Hurting Heart		$17.99	$5.95		
Thoughts From HIS Heart...		$17.99	$5.95		
Thoughts for/21st Century Pastor		$15.99	$5.95		
The Lake of Fire		$16.99	$5.95		
Through Gates of Pearls...		$19.95	$5.95		

Name   Phone:

Address:

Email:

ORDERS PROCESSED & SHIPPED ONCE FULL PAYMENT IS RECEIVED.
PLEASE ADD $5.95 Per Book ordered to cover Shipping & Handling
Please allow 2-6 WEEKS for DELIVERY once payment is received.
EGM Publications special rates are available for bulk orders.

Fill out form and mail your; Certified Check, Cashiers Check, or Money Order to:
Rev. Dr. Eversel M. Griffith • P.O. Box 1177 • Montclair, New Jersey 07042
(NO PERSONAL CHECK PLEASE.)